VIEW LOOKING NORTHEAST IN WATERTOWN, 1886. Many of the buildings in the city put on a pretty façade, when in reality the infrastructures were merely wooden shacks. Many of the people the reader will encounter in this book did the same thing.

Wicked WATERTOWN

HISTORY YOU WEREN'T SUPPOSED TO KNOW

W.F. JANNKE III

THE
History
PRESS

Published by The History Press
Charleston, SC 29403
www.historypress.net

First published 2010

Manufactured in the United States

ISBN 978.1.59629.861.3

Library of Congress Cataloging-in-Publication Data

Jannke, W. F. (William F.)
Wicked Watertown : history you weren't supposed to know / W.F. Jannke, III.
p. cm.
Includes bibliographical references.
ISBN 978-1-59629-861-3
1. Watertown (Wis.)--History--Anecdotes. 2. Watertown (Wis.)--Biography--Anecdotes.
3. Scandals--Wisconsin--Watertown--History--Anecdotes. 4. Corruption--Wisconsin--
Watertown--History--Anecdotes. 5. Watertown (Wis.)--Social life and customs--Anecdotes.
I. Title.

F589.W3J37 2010
977.5'82--dc22
2010009534

CONTENTS

PREFACE

Did you know that H.H. Holmes, America's first documented serial killer, a man who tortured and killed several people in his suburban Chicago home, was known in Watertown? Did you know that Lansing Brown, the accidental killer of 1930s singing sensation Russ Columbo, was a descendant of Timothy Johnson, the founder of Watertown? I wouldn't be surprised if Lizzie Borden had kin who lived in the city as well. These sorts of stories fascinate me, and I hope they will interest you, the reader, as well.

On the following pages, the reader will find many stories of less-than-reputable people and their various misdeeds. I assure the reader from the outset that all the stories you will find are true. They are based on newspaper accounts and public court records.

I have wanted to tell a few of these tales for quite a while, but in Watertown, where my family has resided since the 1840s, the rule of thumb has always been "know the stories but don't tell them." I break all the rules. One of my merriest memories was of an alderman, now since departed from this life, who asked me once why I always dwelled on the darker aspects of the city's history and not its good points. I didn't have a good answer for him then, but I do now: I tell these stories to remind everyone that life in "the good old days" wasn't always that good.

Fortunately, the people you will meet in these pages are the exception, not the rule. The general populace of Watertown are good people, the sorts who will give you the shirt off their back. They enjoy a festival or a sporting event, and they attend church every Sunday. I am proud to call Watertown my home.

The title of this work comes from a letter written in 1893 by a former minister of the First Congregational Church in Watertown, the Reverend B.H. Parsons. He wrote that when he first came to the city in the mid-1840s "the community had the reputation of being a very wicked one." However, the minister went on to write that though things may have been bad at first, by the end of his time here Watertown had become a fine place to live and raise children. A wise man once said that every man has a light and a dark side. These are the stories of man's (and woman's) darker side. If there is a lesson to be learned from their stories it is to never stray from the right path.

I wish to thank Mrs. Patricia Groth and her daughter Charlotte, along with Steve Hackbarth and Ken Riedl, for looking over the manuscript and making valuable suggestions. I also wish to thank the following for use of images: St. Marks Lutheran Church, Joan Ebert, the *Watertown Daily Times*, Mary Rohr, Mary Beggan Mueller, John Reichardt, John Hart and the Watertown Historical Society. All other images come from the personal collection of the author. Finally, I would like to thank Ernst and Yvonne Duesterhoeft for their technical assistance in getting the manuscript into the proper format for the publisher. Thank you, one and all.

I wish to dedicate this volume to Reuben Feld, historian, teacher and entertainer. He taught me that there is more to history than what I learned in grade school and there was more to Watertown history than the Octagon House.

Chapter 1
LAW AND ORDER

Watertown, Wisconsin, lies in the midst of the Rock River Valley. It is located forty-five minutes from the state capital, Madison, and about the same distance from the state's largest city, Milwaukee. Watertown is about three hours from Chicago. The city's fortunate location has always been one of its chief selling points and caused it to be a sort of "jumping-off" place for early immigrants heading for locations in the interior of the state.

The bulk of the city lies within Jefferson County, with the exception of the northernmost section, which lies in Dodge County. Division Street, which is located east of the Rock River, is the dividing line between the two counties. There was a widespread belief that if one committed a crime in Jefferson County, all that person need do was hop over Division Street and wind up in Dodge County and thus escape the officials in the other county. Such is not the case!

The city boasts a population of over twenty-two thousand and is home to America's first kindergarten and astronaut Dan Brandenstein. It is a city of diverse industries, from automatic coin counters to metal products. The majestic Rock River lazily runs through the city, dividing it in half. At one time, it was believed that the rich lived on the east side and those of lesser means lived on the west, but there is really no distinction, and beautiful homes can be found in all areas of the city.

The earliest settlers were Yankees, or "Yorkers," who made their way to this area in the 1830s. They were quickly followed by the Irish and the

Germans, who were, in turn, followed by the Bohemians, Welsh and other ethnic groups, though the Germans far outnumbered every other group that came to the city.

Each group that came to Watertown brought its own beliefs and codes of honor. The early settlers knew that they needed a system of laws and law enforcers, and as early as 1838 there were a sheriff and deputy sheriff who kept the peace in Jefferson County. The early settlers were mainly bachelors seeking to make their fortunes in the New West, and also there were shadowy figures hoping to escape creditors or the law and make a new beginning. This class included horse thieves and counterfeiters. It was a rough life being a pioneer.

The arrival of foreign-speaking immigrants was another cause for concern among the English-speaking settlers here. These newcomers took jobs held formerly by earlier settlers and even had the gall and temerity to court their sisters and daughters! That raised a few hackles, not to mention a few bruises.

These events, coupled with periodic economic depressions of the nineteenth century, prompted outbursts of violence that began to rise in the 1850s and continued on through the remainder of the nineteenth century and into the next. Cases of petty larceny and grand theft began to break out, as well as cases of arson, spousal and child abuse, cruelty to animals, counterfeiting, horse thievery, gambling, rape and prostitution. All these types of crimes made their first appearances in Watertown within the span of the first ten to fifteen years of the city's history.

The local newspaper, the *Watertown Chronicle*, editorialized on August 6, 1851, about the lawlessness of the area. The editor, Jonathan Hadley, wrote: "Watertown is by no means more notorious for lawlessness than other parts of Wisconsin. Hardly an exchange paper comes to us that does not contain a statement of some act of villainy perpetuated in the vicinity of its location."

What kept Watertown from becoming an unrepentive "sin town" was the fundamental moral sensibility of the citizens, no matter what their ethnicity. Several groups appeared at this time to try to curb the manners and morals of the people. Churches sprouted up to help keep people on the straight and narrow; temperance groups tried (unsuccessfully) to curb excessive drinking; and, more importantly, police forces began to get more organized. But Watertown's police force was still a "Keystone Kops"–style organization, and it would remain so, to lesser degrees, practically until the turn of the twentieth century.

History You Weren't Supposed to Know

The earliest police presence was that of a town constable, and the first duly elected constable was Eli A. Bouton, in 1842. As the city grew, each ward of the city had its own constable, as well as its own justice of the peace, which meant that there was little cohesion. There was a sort of guiding force, known as the city marshal, who was ostensibly supposed to be in charge of keeping the peace for the entire city. In addition, there were night watchmen, whose duties were to keep an eye out not only for crimes but also fires. Besides these forces of law and order there was also the Watertown Rifles, a militia company that was formed by German citizens. The Watertown Rifles was in existence in the 1850s and disbanded at the outbreak of the Civil War.

There were several early law-keepers who took their duties very seriously. There was Joseph Giles, who was famous for his long white beard and his habit of chewing tobacco, which left a distinctly brown streak down the middle of said beard. On one occasion, Giles was in hot pursuit of a local lawbreaker named John McGrail. He chased him through the city until they reached the banks of the river, whereupon McGrail jumped in and swam away. It was the first time a criminal had escaped Giles's clutches. Giles was conversant in the Native American tongue and much respected.

Then there was John Reichardt, known locally as "Put." He was a former bareback rider in a circus in his native Germany but took to the law here in Watertown. Under his watch, the city was very well protected. He got his nickname because he would silently creep up to groups that he suspected were up to no good, tap his truncheon and say, "Put, boys, put!" On one occasion, he arrested a group of boys who had commandeered a boat and were about to deliver them to the local lockup when a runaway team caught his attention and the boys managed to escape.

Then there was the author's great-great-uncle, Donat Kehr, a native of Alsace Lorraine, who was city marshal in the mid-1870s. He was liked by some and reviled by others, particularly by Ashley D. Harger, editor of *Harger's Times*, one of Watertown's many early newspapers. On one occasion, Marshal Kehr arrested a speeder, Louis Kniesel, who was racing his buggy over Main Street bridge. Kehr was within his rights as a city marshal, for this was a punishable offense and one could be fined for speeding over the bridge at that time. Accordingly, he forced Kniesel, a local butcher, to stop and get out of the buggy. For his troubles, Kehr received a royal pummeling from Kniesel, who was drunk. The other local papers all sided with the marshal except Harger, who branded Kehr a villain for picking on the poor offender. Where is the justice?

But despite the many keepers of the peace, the people of Watertown were concerned that this was not enough deterrent to the criminal element. In

JOHN "PUT" REICHARDT. He was considered one of the finest law keepers in the city's history. This image shows the former bareback rider in his old age. *Courtesy of John Reichardt.*

the 1850s, there was a rash of petty thefts, and things got so bad that the local newspaper urged the formation of a "Committee of Vigilance" to help police the town. People were getting tired of thievery and arson, and they looked at their protectors with a distinctly jaundiced eye.

One office was particularly singled out for distrust, and that was the office of night watchman. It came out in a court case in the 1880s that Joseph Jantzen, who was the night watchman for the west side of the city, was caught sleeping on the job by the city marshal, Charles Zautner. But just as Zautner was about to turn him in for dereliction of duty, Jantzen foiled him by handing in his resignation.

The city fathers then appointed Charles Wendtland as night watchman in place of the snoozing Jantzen. But Wendtland was *also* found to be asleep on duty. This time, a spirited member of the public, one Fred Behling, in order to procure evidence of the night watch's disregard for his duties, snuck up to the sleeping lawman and actually *stole* his badge. Wendtland was a man with a silver tongue, and he managed somehow to talk his way out of his predicament and the charge against him was dropped. But the whistle-blower, Behling, was summarily arrested for stealing and placed in the city jail. Fortunately, the charges against him were also dropped.

The problem of where to keep lawbreakers was answered early on in Watertown's history with the establishment of the first jail in the late 1840s. The lockup was located on the northeast corner of North Third and East Main Streets. At that time the jail was reportedly so confining that a prisoner could not stand upright in the cells. The city jail later was located along the Rock River on South First Street, and then in 1885 it was transferred to the city hall, which was located on North First Street. In the mid-1960s, the old city hall building was torn down to make way for a picturesque parking lot. A new municipal building was then erected on Jones Street, where it remains today.

The first steps toward a modern police force in the city came when Herman C. Block was appointed Watertown's first chief of police. Block had been on the force since 1896, and he began to institute modern police methods. Following Chief Block was Charles Pieritz, who served from 1916 to 1930. He, in turn, was followed by Albert N. Quest, a retired Milwaukee police officer. Chief Quest was instrumental in completely overhauling the

CITY HALL. This was the home of the Watertown Police and Fire Departments from 1885 to 1965. Today it is a parking lot.

WATERTOWN POLICE DEPARTMENT, TAKEN IN 1935. This image shows some of the stalwart officers proudly displaying their new bulletproof squad car and firearms.

police department and bringing it up to a new high standard. Sadly, he died of a heart attack while on duty. Quest was followed by Theodore C. Voigt, who later became a special agent for the FBI.

While under the leadership of Chief Quest and Chief Voigt, the Watertown Police Department made great strides toward modern methods. Officer training was improved and equipment was modernized. Today, Watertown can claim that it has one of the finest police departments in southeastern Wisconsin.

Gone are the days of the night watch, ward constables, city marshal and their ilk. In their places are policemen and -women, detective squads and other law enforcement professionals. The methods of law-keeping have changed over the years to keep up with the methods of lawbreakers. What always remains the same is that some people are prone to disturbing the peace.

Chapter 2
CALL ME MADAM

In 1913, the Wisconsin state legislature established a committee to investigate the problems of alcohol abuse and prostitution. This committee, known as the Teasdale Committee, sent out undercover fieldworkers to various cities in Wisconsin, and they reported back to the legislature about the extent of wrongdoings in the state. The results were sobering, indeed. The committee managed to collect enough documentation to demonstrate that while no single woman (or man for that matter) was safe in big cities, they were equally at risk in small backwater towns.

A member of the committee visited Watertown in November 1913 and, after investigating, filed a report that is somewhat shocking to read. The operative reported that at a saloon located at 121 West Main Street there were "on the second floor…plainly furnished rooms that are let out for assignation purposes…rooms are let to couples at $1.00 each, the place is open all night, and this seems to be the only class of trade upstairs, very young girls with men are accommodated here, by common reputation it is a tough sporting resort."

The report concluded with the statement that Watertown, in the opinion of the investigator, was "the worst small town I have ever visited." That last remark is sort of hard to take, especially since Watertown has always been remarkably clever at whitewashing its seamier side. One has to wonder how things got to this point.

BEISNER SALOON. This saloon, located at 121 West Main Street, had rented rooms on the upper floor for purposes of prostitution.

The original settlers had little on their minds other than getting a roof over their heads and a crop in the ground. They had no time to be concerned with sex, even though most of the early inhabitants were bachelors. No doubt, around the fireplace at night, thoughts of sweethearts they had left behind haunted their dreams, but there appeared to be no such thing as a lady of the night or a "soiled dove" out in the wilds of the Wisconsin Territory. Certainly not in Watertown at this time.

But as the city grew, so did the carnal urges of its inhabitants. It would seem odd if there were no mention of bawdy houses or men and women of loose morals in a place as large as Watertown, which, by the mid-1850s, had become the second largest city in Wisconsin.

The newspapers of the time were remarkably silent on this issue. The earliest notice of a "house of assignation" appeared in the *Watertown Chronicle* on August 22, 1849. The article read as follows:

> *Awful warning!—At a filthy house of assignation, a short distance from this village, were congregated, a few nights since, five persons—the reputed husband and wife, and three "visitors," black as well as white. The whiskey cup was circulated freely, and bestial excesses indulged in. Pandemonium-*

like as had been the carousals which had been witnessed before, they were all put to blush by that night's debauch. In less than 48 hours thereafter, the miserable woman and her three "visitors" were in eternity! The husband followed during the week! An awful warning to the transgressors!

This was a stern warning, and it makes one wonder just what exactly went on there that caused the death of five people. Still, this did not deter young rakes (or old ones for that matter) from seeking out female comfort. The 1850s were a boom time in the city, but information regarding prostitution is hard to locate. The first hard information to be found regarding prostitution occurs in 1859, ten years after the newspaper article above. It seems that a Mrs. Margaret Stiehl was arrested for maintaining a house of ill fame located somewhere in the old Third Ward of the city, which now encompasses virtually all of the southwestern section of Watertown.

Mrs. Stiehl turned to a life of prostitution due to the fact that she was left destitute after her husband was hauled away to jail. She was described by some of her neighbors as being a drunkard; she was also described as being insane. On one point everyone agreed: she had a bad repute. She was known to consort with a certain Mrs. DeForest, about whom nothing is known other than that she was of equally bad character.

On one occasion a neighbor, Nelson Barrett, heard cries of distress coming from Mrs. Stiehl's house, and he made his way to the front door. He was about to kick it down and investigate when he heard a man's voice cry out, "I'm going to give it to you!" Realizing that what he heard was, in fact, the sounds of lovemaking and not cries of distress, Barrett wisely turned tail and fled the scene before he was discovered. It is infuriating to the researcher that this case never came to a definitive conclusion, apart from Mrs. Stiehl posting a $300 bond. It is presumed that she packed up and left the city.

The 1860s and 1870s passed without much notice. No records seem to detail any hanky-panky going on, so it either didn't exist or it was so well hidden that it went undetected by the authorities. Besides, there was a major distraction, the Civil War, which took people's minds off sexual encounters. And, it might be added, removed many potential johns from the area. The carnal urge would have to wait until the 1880s, when it returned with a vengeance.

The 1880s ushered in a sudden loosening of morals in the city. Sex reared its ugly head, and the newspapers had a field day. In 1882, for example, one local paper reported that girls in Watertown were reported to be on the "mash." Several of them were known to catch on to strangers, and they

SECOND GRUETZMACHER BROTHEL. This 1953 picture shows the second location of Mary Gruetzmacher's brothel on Milwaukee Street. *John Hart photo.*

"perambulated the back streets" with them. The *Watertown Gazette* reported in 1885 that there was a certain house on the west side of the city where girls as young as twelve years of age were being seduced. A report appeared in a local paper at this time of a fight in the middle of Washington Street, one of the most respectable streets in the city, between two ladies of the night. In Watertown at the time, prostitutes were known as "fly girls," presumably because *they drew them.*

Then, in 1886, the news broke of a major brothel located on the corner of South Seventh and Milwaukee Streets run by Mrs. Mary Gruetzmacher. While her business had been located in several other spots, this area was the one most people associated with Mary and her girls. In February 1886, her house was raided by the Watertown police force. Four customers were inside at the time, but they made good their escape. Mary and one of her girls, Mamie Cole, were not so lucky, and they were arrested and taken before Justice William Stacy, who set Mary's bail at $300. This was promptly paid.

With the closing of her business and the subsequent trial, all manner of news made the papers. People were either pleased that a notorious whorehouse had been closed down or they were disgusted that the police seemed to be picking on a working woman. Politicians, depending on which way the wind was blowing, made the Gruetzmacher case part of their campaigns. The city was abuzz with talk of the upcoming case.

The trial began in March 1886, and several witnesses were called. All agreed that it was common knowledge that Mary Gruetzmacher ran a brothel and employed several girls. Almost all the men who testified mentioned one particular girl who went by the unfortunate nickname of "the Little Jew." All agreed that she was the nastiest whore of them all. She was uncouth and swore. She drank publicly, as did all the girls, and she thought nothing of taking one of her clients to a nearby stable and having relations and, afterward, heeding the call of nature, lifting her skirt and using the same place as a restroom. Most of the witnesses were men who, though they denied ever going there, suspiciously knew a great deal about the place. It was claimed that Mary's place was a popular diversion during the monthly Cattle Fair held in the city.

The one female witness, Mrs. Albertine Kiehlblock, added a note of levity to the proceedings. She testified that she had bought a house from Mary Gruetzmacher that was apparently her old brothel. Mrs. Kiehlblock's new

ORIGINAL GRUETZMACHER BROTHEL LOCATION. This image shows the first location of Mary Gruetzmacher's brothel on South Seventh Street. *John Hart photo.*

house was located across the street from the new headquarters of Mary Gruetzmacher. Mrs. Kiehlblock testified that ever since she moved in she had been disturbed day and night by men, sometimes as many as four or five a day, who mistook her house for Mary's. She stated that she would sometimes no sooner turn away someone at the front door then she would find someone coming in through the back. These events, she said, had made her "very nervous."

Incidentally, this would not be the last time the Kiehlblocks would have trouble with sexual encounters. In 1910, Albertine's daughter, Helen, was coming home from a trip at 10:00 p.m. As she put her key in the lock, she felt a presence. Helen was a nervous type and highly excitable. She made her way into her darkened home and ran into a man. She screamed as loud as she could and ran out the door, followed by the man, followed by a woman, who turned out to be Mrs. Louise Lange, a neighbor. Though badly shaken up, Helen had the presence of mind to grab the man by the arm and demand to know who he was. Mrs. Lange pulled her off of the gentleman, and he got away. Even at the trial, his identity was never made public. The only thing known about him was that he was a highly respected citizen.

Several neighbors appeared on the scene to come to Helen's aid, and together they went into the house and carefully looked around. Upon coming to a small bedroom located in the rear of the house, just off the kitchen, they discovered that a woman's shawl had been pinned up over the entryway. Raising the shawl, they discovered Louise Lange in the act of making the bed. She calmly finished up what she was doing, took down the shawl, wrapped it around her head and shoulders and left the house.

It was later revealed at trial that Louise Lange somehow had broken into the Kiehlblock house and used it as a trysting spot. And it seems as though this was not the first time she had met and had sex with men there. The spirit of Mary Gruetzmacher must have looked down and laughed and laughed.

The Gruetzmacher prostitution trial concluded in August 1886. Mary Gruetzmacher pleaded guilty and paid a fine of $200. But this did not end her career as a flesh-peddler. She continued in business at least through 1888, and by that time she had a competitor, Mrs. Hannah Warner, who was running a brothel on Fourth Street.

What were the decent, God-fearing citizens of Watertown going to do to combat this menace? Where could they turn for redress? Then as now, one place where people with an axe to grind could be heard was in the columns of the local press. Accordingly, a curious notice appeared in the *Watertown Gazette* on December 19, 1888, which read as follows:

CHIEF OF POLICE, SIR—You have no doubt heard of the murders in London by Jack the Ripper. To come to business, I want you, as chief, to close that place on Seventh Street owned by Mary Gruetzmacher, and another place run by a woman named Warner. Now REMEMBER what I say, if you fail to do so, I will commence my work, that will bring terror to the hearts of all prostitutes. I will give you until the 26th of this month. REMEMBER THIS WARNING. Yours, JACK THE RIPPER.

Needless to say, there was no slashing of throats in the city, but the area around South Seventh Street did become known as the "Whitechapel District" in honor of the Ripper's stomping ground in England. Strange things began to take place around this area. Women and children, it was reported, were attacked, and men were robbed. In other parts of town, "Jack the Jumper" began to make an appearance. This menace would hide behind bushes and lie in wait for women who wandered out alone at night. As they passed, he would jump out at them and chase them. The people in Watertown were pretty upset.

But then, strange to say, just as soon as these happenings flared up, they died out, and by the end of the nineteenth century all traces of the brothels near Seventh and Milwaukee Streets, not to mention Fourth Street, seemed to have disappeared. The whitewashing of history had begun.

Then in 1906, twenty years after the Mary Gruetzmacher trial, a new madam appeared on the scene, coincidentally also bearing the name Gruetzmacher. This new brothel-keeper was Mrs. Ida (Buege) Gruetzmacher. She ran a bawdy house on South Fourth Street, between Bailey and Clyman Streets.

But there is nothing remotely amusing about this story. It all revolves around a fourteen-year-old epileptic named Elsie Weichert. She was a simple-minded girl who had only just learned to read and write. But she was an early bloomer, and this made her a target for men on the make. She was first lured into having sex by one August Bandelin, a shoe factory worker. He enticed her to come into the shop one Sunday as she was going to Sunday school. Once inside, he took off her drawers and had her lay on a box, and he had his way with her. He promised the girl that if she came back the next Sunday he would not only give her money, but he would also give her a new pair of shoes. From here, her life began to spiral downward.

We next hear of young Elsie when she was brought to the police station by her mother. She swore to the justice of the peace, W.D. Stacy, that she had been at Ida Gruetzmacher's house and she had been forced to have relations with one Charles Donovan, an itinerant common laborer.

Ida and Charlie were arrested and held in jail. At her trial, Ida maintained her innocence, as did Charlie, but as the facts were told, things looked pretty bad. It seems that Elsie and her mother had often visited with Ida, and Elsie often came to her house alone to help with odd jobs around there. On one of these occasions, Elsie had one of her epileptic fits and began to roll around on the floor, hiking her dress up and exposing her underwear. Ida laughed at this and remarked that she could make a lot of money doing that.

Then in June 1906, Ida demonstrated to the young girl how to pleasure a man by laying on top of Charles Donovan. The following Sunday, which was June 3, Ida took off the young girl's panties and had her lay on the lounge. Donovan laid on top of her, and as Elsie later reported, she thought her "stomach would break" with his weight. For her troubles, the girl was paid a nickel. She was also cautioned not to tell her mother what had happened there, but, of course, the girl did just that.

Ida was found guilty of running a brothel and sentenced to eighteen months in jail. For enticing young Elsie into a life of prostitution, she was sentenced to two years at the Wisconsin State Reformatory. This last charge was later dropped.

Charles Donovan was charged and found guilty of rape and sentenced to eight years at hard labor in the prison at Waupun. He appealed, and his sentence was later reversed. Then the story took a different turn. On New Year's Eve 1906, Donovan broke out of jail, freeing two other prisoners in the bargain. He took off and, two years later, was discovered living in Atlantic, Iowa, where he was apprehended. He was tracked down by means of letters written by a sweetheart of his in Wisconsin.

As for Elsie Weichert, she was committed to the Hospital for the Feeble-Minded in Chippewa Falls in 1907. And so the second Gruetzmacher trial came to an inglorious end.

Other cases came and went very quickly, like the case of a house of ill fame located at 1310 Neenah Street in the southeastern part of the city that sprang up in 1913, about the same time as the Teasdale Committee. This house was kept by Mrs. Bertha Klatt and her lover, William Bowman. On a drizzly and dreary night in February 1913, the Klatt home was besieged by a group of rowdies who were pelting the house with stones and pails—anything that came to hand.

Into this morass came a group of thrill-seeking young gentlemen: Robert Strehlow, Ernie Neitzel, Herman Schultz and William Polzin. They had been drinking, and as they were all about to go home, one of them convinced the others to go down to Bertha's to see what a real brothel was like. They arrived just before the crowd of rowdies did. The men tried to get Bertha to come out, but she refused. They were about to leave when the others arrived and began a general disturbance. One of the rowdies took the little group of young men down to the cellar to show them where Bertha would have sex with her customers. The basement was empty save for a small pile of excelsior on the floor near a corner. They left soon after and were making their way up the street when they heard gunshots.

Bertha had gotten frightened for her life and summoned her lover, Bowman, to come to her rescue. Seizing a rifle from her dresser, which she kept for her protection, she loaded it with birdshot and handed it to Bowman. He shot once through the screen door. Bertha then grabbed it and shot it herself. The crowd scattered, and another shot, apparently from Bowman, came again. This one hit Robert Strehlow in the left shoulder.

The next day, Bowman and Klatt were arrested. Bowman was charged with assault with a deadly weapon and fined $100 plus court costs. Klatt was charged with keeping a house of ill fame and fined $100 plus court costs.

With the closing of the Klatt brothel, the city circled the wagons and tried to put a liberal coat of whitewash on things. But "the world's oldest profession" couldn't be kept down, and from time to time the press reported on strange goings-on at places such as area roadhouses. The courts had a field day with the events surrounding a rather notorious "resort" that was being run on the city's eastern border in which a father forced his entire family into the "profession" in the late 1930s.

This made the story of the local woman who lived near one of Watertown's parochial schools look like the story of Pollyanna. All she did, after all, was to put a different-colored light in her window each night to tell a particular suitor when he could call.

The last time prostitution was mentioned in the Watertown press was in the 1980s, when the police force raided a local bar and arrested a number of "call girls." Today it is difficult to track down any records of prostitution in Watertown. No doubt the profession still thrives, but the operators today are a lot more careful in how they conduct themselves.

Still, where there's a will, very often one can procure a Jill.

Chapter 3

A DEATH IN THE FAMILY

The cry of murder, even in these jaded times when one is bombarded on a daily basis by scenes of killings and other atrocities on television and on the Internet, is still greeted with dread. It is still a comparatively rare occurrence in Watertown, even though there was a major murder case in each decade from the 1850s through to the end of the nineteenth century. There were, of course, several cases in the twentieth century and even today, but the number still does not compare with the large-scale killings in large urban areas such as Milwaukee or Madison.

Murders are virtually always senseless and violent, and it is hard to differentiate between what is the more heinous type of murder. For this work, we will discuss the cases where family members turned on other members and committed patricide (the killing of one's father) and matricide (the killing of one's mother) and declare that as far as murders go, these are among the worst sorts. As Shakespeare wrote, "How sharper than a serpent's tooth is an ungrateful child," and while the following cases, for the most part, do not concern themselves with ungrateful children, the remark is still apropos.

The earliest murder to take place in Watertown was the Kuntz patricide of 1851. The murder actually did not take place within the city of Watertown itself, but rather occurred in the town of Watertown, in an area southwest of the city. On the morning of April 28, 1851, Peter Inglehart, a neighbor

The West Road, circa 1873. This road leading southwest out of Watertown will take one past the Kuntz and Schnepf murder sites.

of the Kuntz family, made his way over to see them. He no doubt felt a trifle uneasy because of the many strange reports he had heard recently of the family. A son, Christopher Kuntz Jr., had recently been shot square in the face while in the act of trying to force his way into a nearby house on a "maniac whim." And one of the daughters of the family, Katharine, had run away from home and sought refuge at a neighbor's house due to the goings-on at her home, so it took a certain amount of courage for Inglehart to seek out the family on his own.

When he arrived at the Kuntz farm, a strange sight met his eyes. An article in the *Watertown Chronicle* described it as follows: "Mr. Inglehart... found the ground about the house strewn with bedding, clothing, etc., the mother wandering about talking incoherently, and the son [Christopher Jr.] on a bed outside and near the door."

Undeterred by these sights, Inglehart pushed his way through the debris, went up to a broken window on the house and looked inside. What he saw there made his hair stand on end. There, lying in the midst of still more

DR. JAMES CODY. He was the Watertown physician brought in to examine the body of murder victim Christopher Kuntz Sr.

debris, was the body of Christopher Kuntz Sr., dead. The *Chronicle* went on to describe the body, which was

> *entirely naked, covered with bruises and drawn into the closest and most compact possible state, with ropes and chains, and presenting a…shocking and unsightly appearance…cords were bound tightly around the wrists and ankles, and a heavy log chain passed around the neck and drawn through the cords, and the whole body, thus, with the chains drawn together. The lower portions of the legs were then brought tightly up to the body, by cords passed around them and the hips…two of the lower ribs were broken—the face bruised and blackened, with one eye broken out, and a wound in the skull penetrating to the brain.*

After seeing this terrible sight, Inglehart ran off to fetch help. Little by little the news leaked out that a murder had taken place at the Kuntz farm, and all day long a parade of neighbors came over to gawk at the dead man. Finally, the authorities arrived from Watertown, and after making an examination, they placed a sheet over the corpse. Dr. James Cody, a leading Watertown physician, observed that the deceased was so tightly bound up that he didn't think it was possible for a human to do that without mechanical means.

Mother and son each admitted to killing the old man, and they—along with another son, Adam—were taken into custody and brought to the jail in

JEFFERSON COUNTY COURTHOUSE. This is where most of the cases found in this book were heard, including the Kuntz and Schnepf murder cases.

Watertown. The next day, they were transferred to the county jail in nearby Jefferson to await their trial.

How did things come to this? How did Christopher Kuntz Sr. meet his fate? On the surface, they seemed to be no different from other German immigrant families. They had left the old country and arrived in America in the late 1840s. Like most immigrants, they were, no doubt, in search of a better life in the New World.

The Kuntz family entered the United States through the Port of New Orleans and traveled to Wisconsin via steamboat up the Mississippi. The family, when they arrived, was composed of Christopher Kuntz Sr.; his wife, Maria Katharine; two daughters, Katharine and Mary Margarethe; and three sons, the oldest of whom were Christopher Jr., and Adam. Not much is known about the third son, as he disappeared as the family was traveling to Wisconsin. Whether he wandered too near the side of the boat and fell into the water and drowned or whether he was spirited away, no one ever quite knew. But suspicion always seemed to fall on the father, Christopher Sr., as being the culprit, though why he would have wished to do harm to his son is unknown. Still, the belief persisted, especially in the mind of his wife, and things began to go downhill.

Once in Wisconsin, the family bought from the U.S. government about eighty acres of land (located today along what is known as Clifford Lane, just off the West Road, southwest of Watertown) and commenced to erect a house and get a crop in. According to the 1850 Census, the family lived in a small one-room cabin and owned two cows, two bulls, a quantity of lumber and the crops in the field. The entire value of their real and personal property amounted to $445.

The two older boys, Adam and Christopher Jr., hired themselves out to other farms in the area and lived away from home, leaving Mr. and Mrs. Kuntz and their daughters alone at the house. Mrs. Kuntz began to deteriorate mentally under the pressures of life in the New World. Though they lived in a fairly populated area, their nearest neighbor was several miles away. Thus, left alone to do nothing but the same work day in, day out, she became unhinged and began to believe that her husband had killed their little boy. As for Mr. Kuntz, the strain of having to live with a wife who was slowly losing her reason began to affect his mental state as well.

What happened next, incredibly, was spelled out in the pages of the *Watertown Chronicle* by two writers who signed themselves "A" and "Z." These two armchair sleuths presented their views of the event in hopes of casting a light on a frontier tragedy and quelling the many rumors that were running rife throughout the countryside.

Writer "A" argued that what happened to the Kuntz family was due to insanity induced by "religious zealotry." The writer claimed that the old man had been a religious skeptic or "rationalist" and because of this lack of faith he had been subjected to continuous proselytizing by members of the German Methodist Church in Watertown. This had the effect of driving the old man insane.

As a result of the old man's insanity, the entire family began to have delusions brought on by religious frenzy, and ultimately they all, too, went mad. Soon the entire family became convinced that the old man had killed his son on the riverboat. In the weeks leading up to the murder, the father became violent and his sons had to restrain him. Supposedly, according to Writer "A," the old man then ordered his sons to tie him up and beat him as an act of repentance. While in the heat of the moment, Christopher Jr. lost control and wound up beating his father to death. "A" summed up his view by stating that the guilty needed pity, not punishment, and suggested that the court should give them a light sentence.

Writer "Z" took an opposite look at the case and stated that the Kuntz family had suspected the old man of killing his son from the start. According to this writer, the event that tipped the scales occurred when Mrs. Kuntz saw a young boy in the neighborhood who bore an uncanny resemblance to her lost son. This opened the floodgates and pushed Maria Katharine Kuntz over the edge. She openly began to blame her husband for killing their son and often tried to attack him. Christopher Jr., having been the one to always keep the peace and restrain his parents from harming each other, began to lose his grip on reality, and this led to his wandering into a neighbor's house and being shot. It soon became apparent that the entire family was gripped by insanity. "Z" went on to write that it was Mrs. Kuntz who demanded that her son, Christopher Jr., tie up the old man and beat him to death. Writer "Z" concluded his letter by stating that the punishment should fit the crime. The writer also went out of his way to refute the charge that the German Methodists had anything to do with the case, inadvertently tipping his hand that he might have been a member of said church.

Mrs. Kuntz and her son were each charged with five counts of murder. The other son, Adam, was released. The case had been held over until the fall term of the circuit court, so Christopher and his mother cooled their heels in the county jail until then. Their case was handled by Daniel Weymouth, a prominent Jefferson lawyer. One of the first things he did was appoint an administrator to manage the Kuntz farm and to find homes for the two little girls who had been staying with their brother Adam at the farm. These two girls had been terrified of the place since the murder and claimed that "the old man's ghost haunts the house." They were boarded out with neighbors.

The trial finally got underway at Jefferson on October 30, 1851. The proceedings were swift, and the cases for the prosecution and the defense were over by 8:00 p.m. On October 31, the case was handed over to the jury, which took a mere fifteen minutes to make its decision. Maria Katharine Kuntz, wife of the deceased, was found not guilty and immediately released. Christopher Kuntz Jr. was found "not guilty by reason of insanity," and he was bound over for further examination and ultimately released into the custody of his relatives. His mother and brother, Adam, were required to post a $500 bond to guarantee that Christopher Jr. would be "well and severally kept."

Thus ended the first major murder case in Watertown's history and, interestingly, one of the earliest uses of the temporary insanity defense in the state of Wisconsin. As for the Kuntz family, they returned to the homestead. The murder was forgotten. The girls later married local men and left home. The boys prospered and grew to ripe old ages.

Sixteen years after the Kuntz murder, another patricide case occurred not too far from the 1851 murder site. There must have been a curse on this area to have had not one, but two such cases within a short span of time. This next case occurred on April 3, 1867.

It was a drizzly day. Charles Schnepf, a veteran of the recent Civil War, and his son Joseph had risen early and gone off to a nearby field to cut stove wood and to collect and burn brush so that the fields could be cleared in the coming weeks.

There had been bad blood between father and son for some time. The cause was simple: Charles wanted his son to follow in his footsteps and be a farmer, but his son wanted to leave the farm and try his hand at a profession in the city. The father could be quarrelsome, was prone to mood swings and, on top of all that, was a drinker. When he was intoxicated, he could become violent. His wife knew just how bad it could be, because just before he left for the war he had signed over his farm to his wife in the event that he was killed. Charles returned unscathed and demanded his wife sign the farm back over to him. She refused, and an ugly quarrel began, which resulted in his throttling her. Young Joe, trying to protect his mother, stepped in, pointed a revolver at his father and fired. Thankfully, the pistol misfired and no one was hurt. After that, an uneasy truce was declared by all parties. But by the time of the murder, things were peaceful, and Charles Schnepf had even gone so far as to promise to set his son up in a trade. Then came the fatal day.

At his hearing and later at his trial, Joe Schnepf told the story of that day as follows: He and his father had gone to the field to collect and burn brush piles and bring back stove wood. While they were engaged in this activity, the old man, with a wild look in his eye, suddenly announced that he was going to go to Watertown to get some tobacco and see about some seed wheat. Joe thought this was an odd thing for him to do, especially since Charles was not wearing a warm coat, but as the old man was prone to unpredictable actions he thought nothing of it.

The last thing Charles Schnepf said to his son was that he should be sure to burn the brush piles that day. When Joe tried to argue that it was too wet for a fire to properly burn, his father became insistent, and Joe, wishing to keep the peace, agreed to do the job. Joseph then watched as his father went off through the woods toward Watertown. It was the last time he would see his father.

After getting half the work done, Joe returned home for lunch. After the meal, he took his little sister and the family dog and returned to the field to continue the brush collection. The last thing he did was set fire to the pile, and after watching the flames for a while, they all returned home. There they performed their evening chores, had supper and afterward had a singalong around the hearth. Then Joe went out and tended the stock, and by 11:00 p.m. the entire family was fast asleep.

Not a one seemed too disturbed that Charles Schnepf had not returned home. In fact, nearly four days passed before the thought that something had happened to the old man occurred to anyone. And when that thought did occur, it was the neighbors who thought it. Knowing the bad blood that existed between Joe and his father, the neighbors decided to check up on things.

Accordingly, a group converged on the farm to search for Mr. Schnepf. They searched the house from attic to cellar and the farm yard but found no trace of the old man. They did, however, notice that Joseph seemed to be acting a little too unconcerned about his father's disappearance. In fact, he told people that he didn't think his father would return and tried to sell them his father's reaper. Joe also seemed to be leading the search party away from the site where his father had last been seen.

When they finally searched the field where Charles was last seen, the crowd made an unpleasant discovery. There, amidst the ashes of the brush heap, were found charred bones, suspender clips and shoe nails. The first conclusion that everyone jumped to was that Charles Schnepf had been killed and his body burned on the ash heap. But who had killed him? Given the way Joe had been acting, their suspicions turned toward the son, and they seized him. Young Joe tried to plead his innocence, but the crowd was whipped into a frenzy at the thought of a son turning on his father. He was held until the authorities could arrive to transport him to jail. While he was incarcerated there was talk of a lynching.

From jail, Joseph wrote a series of pathetic letters to friends and family pleading his innocence and praying to God to protect him. In one letter he wrote that he hoped "my Deare Father will come back…and get us poor creatures out of trouble. My hart is frea and lite because God knows that I am inisent [innocent] and cleare and that keeps qurrage [courage] up every time."

Fearing that he wouldn't get a fair trial in Jefferson, the case was moved to Portage, Wisconsin, which is located in the central part of the state. It began in December 1867. The entire trial testimony was printed in both the *Watertown Democrat* and its rival, the *Watertown Republican*. It made for salacious reading.

The trial lasted a mere nine days. Each side produced a bevy of witnesses, but from the start the prosecution's case, which had been built on circumstantial evidence at best, seemed to be the weaker of the two. Of the doctors they produced to try to establish whether the bones found at the ash pile were those of Charles Schnepf, neither could agree that they were even human bones and not animal bones.

Once the case was turned over to the defense, the prosecution's case was completely destroyed by three pivotal witnesses. The first witness was Professor Carr of Madison, who claimed that it was virtually impossible for a human body to be so completely consumed by an open fire as the remains presented into evidence. He claimed that in order for that to have occurred someone would have had to have kept the fire going at full tilt for several days, and there were no witnesses who appeared on the stand to support this assertion. Even Joseph's whereabouts were all accounted for.

The next witness called was Mrs. Mary Kniesel, the wife of a Watertown butcher. She swore under oath that she had seen Charles Schnepf walk past her shop three days *after* his supposed death. The third witness called was Catherine Meyers, whose testimony drew everyone's attention to a recent case of suicide that had a great deal of bearing on the case at the bar. This witness was a daughter of Frank Meyers, a neighbor of the Schnepf family and of the man who had committed suicide. There had been a long-standing feud between Meyers and Schnepf that was the result of Meyers's hogs getting into Schnepf's grains one harvest season. Charles took the animals back to their owner, but they soon returned, and this led to bad blood. Meyers was the more aggressive of the two combatants.

Catherine testified that lately her father had begun to show signs of mental aberration. She claimed that it was the result of his taking quack medicines for health problems and that these medicines affected his brain. He acted out in very peculiar ways and got it into his head that Yankee soldiers were going to swoop down on them and kill them all. In order to prevent "them" from getting their hands on his money, he began to give large sums away. He even went so far as to move furniture from the house into the barn to make sure that when "they" came to burn down the house his possessions would be safe. A neighbor, Charles Kohlmetz, was also called to the stand, and he corroborated all that Catherine had said.

Catherine was recalled, and she stated that just before her father hanged himself he said to her something that disturbed her greatly. Frank Meyers told his daughter that soon he would take poor Charlie Schnepf's place and then Schnepf could go to heaven. This statement, the defense asserted, amounted to an admission of guilt. It was theorized that Meyers met Schnepf in the forest and they exchanged words, and one thing led to another and Meyers killed his neighbor and burned his body.

The jury received its instructions on December 11, 1867, and retired to deliberate at 4:00 p.m. After a mere fifteen minutes, the members returned with a verdict of "not guilty." The *Watertown Democrat* reported that after the verdict was announced, "the little brother was passed over the railing to the prisoner and embraced…with childish happiness. Then came the sisters and mother and, with tears shining from eyes long used to weeping, they embraced mother and son."

After the trial, the family returned to the homestead. Shortly afterward, Joseph wrote the editor of the *Watertown Democrat* a letter in which he asked to be left alone so that he could once more resume his old life. He wrote,

> *I do not <u>fear</u> to go, and do not in publishing this statement wish to be understood as asking anybody's <u>permission</u> to go. I merely wish to reason with your better judgment, and to ask that all my old neighbors who have testified that previous to the time I was arrested for murdering and hurting my father, I was a good boy and should, now that I am acquitted of the charge, after a fair trial, <u>let me alone</u>.*

He went on to assure his neighbors that "I do not think there is the least probability that I shall molest anybody or nuisance anyone in word or deed."

He finished his letter by stating, "If people don't want to associate or talk with me, it is at least due me that I be allowed the <u>silent</u> contempt and scornful aversion of those who were once so fiercely in favor of lynching me."

The family continued to live on their farm through the 1870s, when most of the land sold off. As for Joseph, it appears that he left the area sometime after 1873 for parts unknown. One interesting side note to this case involves a character witness called on behalf of young Joseph. This witness was Adam Kuntz, the same person who was at one time implicated in the murder of his own father in 1851. Some witness!

Murdering one's father is a horrible crime, but the killing of one's mother is truly heinous. There has been, to date, only one case of matricide in the history of Watertown, but that one was enough. It happened in the northern part of the city on a bitterly cold day in 1882.

On December 7, 1882, the authorities were called to the home of John and Barbara Kodesch. There they found the body of John's ninety-five-year-old mother, Mary, lying on a bed near the stove in the kitchen. She was dead. But how did she meet her fate?

The family lived on a farm containing twenty-five acres. It was not much of a place, for after the trial the property was sold off and netted little over $2,000 for the real estate and only $10 for the personal goods. John was a weak, good-for-nothing drinker who was ruled by his wife, Barbara. The couple had three daughters. John's mother also made her home with them.

Well, "made her home" may not have been quite true. She was forced to sleep in the barn among the animals. She was a bone of contention in the family, and John and his wife often argued about her. The old lady was treated shamefully. She was dressed in rags and was forced to go barefoot year-round. Neighbors reported seeing mother and son arguing at the top of their lungs in the front yard, and on one occasion he offered ten dollars to anyone who would kill his mother so he was rid of her. The family had even tried to have her sent to the poor farm, but the officials of the poor farm refused to take her.

So the old lady was forced to stay with a family that was at best indifferent to her and at worst abused her horribly. Things finally came to a head in 1882. John and his wife had been arguing more than usual about the old lady on the days leading up to the murder. On the day of the murder, John acted very nervously, as though he sensed something was about to happen. That night after supper, Mary Kodesch retired to her straw pallet in the barn. Shortly after she left, Barbara Kodesch followed her out. It would be the last time Mary Kodesch would be seen alive.

The next day, Barbara was the first one up, followed by her husband and daughters. She went out to check on her mother-in-law and soon came running back into the kitchen crying, "Oh Jesus! Grandmother is dead!" The family all ran out to the barn and found the bruised and bloodied body of Mary Kodesch lying underneath a feather tick. They carried her into the house and laid her in a bed near the stove. John and Barbara told their daughters not to say anything about their grandmother sleeping in the barn. They were to tell anyone who asked that she always slept in the house. Then they dispatched the girls to fetch the authorities.

When the officials finally arrived and made their examination of the deceased, they discovered that though she was bruised (Barbara would later claim that a horse must have kicked her mother-in-law), she did not die from a beating. She *froze to death*. But how did a woman who, as they were assured, always slept in a warm house freeze to death? It was then that John and Barbara Kodesch told those assembled that the old lady preferred to sleep in the barn. Given the choice between a house filled with hate and a barn, who could blame her?

Suspicions were aroused, and John Kodesch and his wife were arrested and charged with the murder of Mary Kodesch. At the trial their daughters, in exchange for immunity, gave damaging testimony. Soon the public knew all the particulars about how the aged woman was ill treated by her family. Through it all, John and his wife maintained their innocence.

In a pathetic attempt to gain sympathy with the jury, Barbara Kodesch feigned a bout of temporary deafness, which soon was found to be a blatant lie. Then John Kodesch, in a fit of despondency, tried to commit suicide in his cell. Public opinion turned against them, as did the jury, which rendered a verdict of guilty against them both.

John and Barbara Kodesch were each sentenced to life imprisonment in the State Prison at Waupun. Their three daughters watched, emotionless, as their parents were hauled away in the patrol wagon to begin their sentence. John died a few years later. His wife tried to commit suicide in jail sometime later but was unsuccessful in her attempt. Thus, the case came to a close.

Chapter 4

I DON'T WANT TO SET THE WORLD ON FIRE

The cry of "Fire!" sends chills down the spines of most people. The loss of property and life can be, and often is, enormous. There were many fires in the city, two of which very nearly wiped out the city's Main Street in 1862 and again in 1865. These fires, like most, were accidental. But not all fires are the result of carelessness or accidents. Some fires are set deliberately either to recover insurance monies or to punish another party, or in rare cases to gratify some inner, almost sexual, desire to see flames licking away at a structure. These types of cases are arson cases, and Watertown has often been plagued with cases such as these.

Arson was easy to pull off in the nineteenth century when everything was made of wood and fire departments were ill equipped and badly organized. Watertown had not one but two fire departments, one for the Irish and one for the Germans, so the rumors went. By the mid-1800s, each fire department boasted a fine, steam-powered pumping engine and many willing volunteers. Still, they could only do so much, and fires still claimed many buildings.

Perhaps the worst case of arson ever to take place in the city, at least in the nineteenth century, occurred in 1890, and it involved two young boys, Eddie Weigel and Johnnie Schlueter. Not much is known about Eddie's background except that he lived in the vicinity of the city hall on North First Street.

As for Johnnie, he was the son of Nicholas and Leopoldina Schlueter. He was a typical thirteen-year-old boy and was, at least by the standards of the

PHOENIX FIREHOUSE, CIRCA 1877. Built in 1876, this was the second fire department located on the west side of the river. It merged with the Pioneer Fire Company in 1912 to form the Watertown Fire Department. *Courtesy of Watertown Historical Society.*

day, well cared for by his parents in a loving but stern manner. He tried their patience, however, because of his refusal to attend school and stay on the straight and narrow.

Of the two boys, it would seem that the younger one, Eddie, was by far more skilled in the ways of the street than his older cohort. Eddie began his criminal ways early on. As a student at St. Henry's Catholic School, he used to steal his schoolmates' lunch pails at recess. As for Johnnie, about the only major quirk he showed was the odd habit of sleeping in a wooden box of wood shavings on the front lawn of his home. He claimed that he preferred that to going indoors and getting "licked" for not attending school.

Granted, these were not typical goings-on, but since they were boys, these little traits were overlooked. At least they weren't out vandalizing, like the group of boys who spread pitch on the outer walls of the Methodist church in the city in the 1880s; and thank heavens they weren't playing with guns. The newspapers of the time were rife with articles concerning young children who managed to get their hands on firearms carelessly left lying about by thoughtless parents. Invariably, these children managed to shoot off a digit or maim one another to the point where it remains a matter of profound wonder that anyone survived childhood without a major bullet wound. Remember, guns don't kill people. Bullets do.

No, the only thing Eddie and Johnnie liked to do was flaunt the city curfew and stay out late with their friends on the streets. If this was all they ever did, their names would have been lost to history.

G.B. LEWIS PLANT, 1891. This engraving shows the Lewis plant a year after the place was burned down by John Schlueter and Eddie Weigel. *Courtesy of Watertown Historical Society.*

But then, the fires started.

They began big, with the destruction of the Lewis and Parks Bee Ware and Box Factory on South Water Street in April 1890, and from there moved on to a livery stable and several barns before their rampage came to an end. Never before had the city been hit with a serial firebug, and no doubt fears ran high among property owners. Who would be next? There had been no loss of life up until now, but that could easily change.

Strangely, though, with the burning of a barn located just off North First Street belonging to John P. Herzog, a harness maker and saloonkeeper (coincidentally in the same neighborhood that Eddie Weigel lived in), the fires came to a stop. Actually, just about all the fires took place in a fairly concentrated area.

No one dared think the siege was over, but there did seem to be a reprieve in the damage. But *who* was responsible? Charles Parks, co-owner of the ruined box factory, offered a private reward for the arrest of the culprit who burned down his building, but no one came forth to claim it.

Then, in the fall of 1890, a break came in the case. A youth was arrested for stealing a pocket watch from a local jeweler, and the youthful offender was hauled before Justice J.C. Halliger. The thief was none other than Eddie Weigel.

Eddie was quite a busy boy. In between robberies, he had attempted to burn down St. Henry's Catholic Church in a most diabolical way. He took lamp oil from the church and sprinkled it along the floor. Then he threw match heads on the floor so that when someone would walk up the aisle, that person would strike the matches and light the oil, thus setting the church ablaze.

He was caught in the act by one of the priests, and when questioned, he confessed all. But despite this, Justice Halliger, who was apparently as blind as the statue of justice itself, dismissed all of that and instead focused mainly on the boy's thievery and sent him to the reform school in Waukesha.

Eddie was accompanied to the school by Deputy Sheriff Herman Graewe. As the deputy was about to leave, Eddie was suddenly seized with an attack of honesty, and he admitted setting fires to the Lewis-Parks box factory, the George Evans livery barn, a barn belonging to Edward Leschinger and a barn belonging to John Herzog, all in Watertown, and all committed between April and May 1890. He also implicated Johnnie Schlueter in the crimes.

Deputy Graewe dismissed this confession as the attention-getting act of a remorseful boy, but when Charles Parks got wind of it, something told him that Eddie was telling the truth. So he went over to Waukesha, and in the presence of the "keeper" of the school, William H. Sleep, he quizzed Eddie about the box factory fire. The story Eddie told him at the reform school and later at the trial ran like this:

Eddie and Johnnie Schlueter had been hanging out together all day. They had discussed setting fire to something and finally hit on the Lewis-Parks plant. They would wait until the electric streetlights went out, which was after midnight, and then they would make their move.

The boys hid out in the Weber Lumber Yard across the street and kept an eye on the factory. The plant had no night watchman, as it was busy round the clock. There were different shifts of workers always on the premises. Being a woodenware factory, there were lots of wood shavings. These were regularly collected in bins and dumped into an area underneath the factory. There was an outside door to this basement room, and Eddie and Johnny knew this.

At the agreed-upon time, the boys made their way over to the factory. Now Eddie claimed that Johnnie went into the room under the factory, while Johnnie always maintained that Eddie went into the room. Whoever it was, the boys ultimately found themselves in that basement room, which was filled with shavings and sawdust, both highly combustible materials. Here each of them lit a match, threw them into the shavings pile and then ran off back to their hiding place in the lumberyard to watch the fun.

It wasn't too long before flames began to appear at the door. Soon, smoke began to fill the factory. The workmen began to panic. They raced out of the building and watched helplessly as the flames consumed not only the Lewis-Parks plant but the Chapman Woolen Mills located directly to the south of the Lewis factory as well. When the flames were finally doused, there was nothing left. The total loss of the Lewis plant was estimated between $30,000 and $35,000.

Meanwhile, the boys, watching the fire engines and the men, had had their fill of the excitement and quietly made their way out of the lumberyard, went west up East Madison Street to South Washington Street and hid out in a barn somewhere near the home of Lieutenant Governor Jesse Stone. There they spent the rest of the night. In the morning, they made their way back to their respective homes.

Parks, who always maintained that he used no coercion on his part in talking to Eddie, proceeded to swear out a complaint against Johnnie Schlueter, who was subsequently arrested. At the trial, Johnnie was alternately crying and sick to his stomach, while Eddie, on the other hand, remained remarkably composed. People began to feel sorry for young Schlueter. It was revealed that his father often beat him and had wanted him to be sent to the reform school mainly because he wouldn't attend the local school.

At the trial, the boys were asked why they set these fires in the first place, and each one said that he had done it merely because "they wanted to see a really good fire!"

Ultimately, the case went to the jury, and after due deliberations they returned a verdict of guilty. Johnnie Schlueter was sentenced to the reform school in Waukesha where Eddie was already serving time, thus bringing to an end the string of arson fires that had plagued the city.

Or did it? In 1892, Johnnie was released from the reform school and returned to Watertown. Not long after his return, a new series of fires began, starting with the E.W. Schultz furniture store located on the northwest corner of West Main and North Water Streets and culminating in several attempts at trying to burn the barbershop belonging to W.J. Lee. The *Watertown Gazette* ran the following notice on October 7, 1892:

IS THERE A FIRE BUG IN THE CITY? Since the burning of E.W. Schultz's furniture store several attempts have been made to burn the building occupied by W.J. Lee as a barber shop on the west side, the last attempt being made on last Sunday evening, a bunch of rags saturated with kerosene being found under the shed of the rear of the building. John Schlueter, the boy sent to reform school over a year ago is back in the city again, and it is said was heard to give "pointers" to a companion who desires to become an inmate of that institution, telling him "all you have to do is to set fire to a building and they will send you there—you can learn a trade, become educated and get plenty to eat." If this is true, the quicker the young lad is returned to the reform school the better. He is a dangerous person to have in the city. This advice may have been the cause of the late fires. It needs to be investigated.

Perhaps the most senseless and savage case of arson took place in the town of Watertown in 1921. In the town of Watertown there is a road known as the Coffee Road, named, so the story goes, because of the smell of coffee that wafted out of the homes of the German farmers living in this area. Strange things happen in the country, but nothing is stranger than what happened to Leona Schlosser.

On the night of August 9, 1921, at 11:00 p.m., Leona Schlosser, the young wife of farmer Max Schlosser, stepped outside after hearing a noise. Before she could make a sound she was set upon by three unknown assailants. They grabbed her from behind and forced her to her knees. They then proceeded to cut off her hair with a sharp instrument. They then ordered the shocked

MAX AND LEONA SCHLOSSER. This is a picture of the young couple who were menaced by unknown assailants in 1921. *Courtesy of* Watertown Daily Times.

woman to get back into the house, cautioning her to "keep mighty still or we will cut off your head!" Owing to her highly excited state, she was unable to identify the men who attacked her.

Bloodied and shaken, she staggered back into the house and summoned her husband. Max listened to her hysterical story, and when she had finished he fetched his gun. Running out into the yard to confront the villains, Max saw some retreating figures and shot at them. Then he returned to his badly shaken wife and they retired.

The Schlossers had been married for about three years and were living on a farm owned by Mrs. Schlosser's uncle, Adolph Knaack. Besides the young couple, a baby and a nine-year-old niece of Mrs. Schlosser were in the house on the night of the attack.

Not long after the Schlossers retired, they smelled smoke, and to their horror it was discovered that their house, which was of log construction, was on fire. Neighbors rushed over to help the young couple. Together they managed to save much of the furnishings, but the house was a total loss. The next morning, it was discovered that the family dog had perished in the flames as well. Other than that, all escaped safely.

Even before the embers cooled, rumors began to spread about the cause of the fire. Some felt it may have been set to cash in on the insurance, but since the house did not belong to the Schlossers but rather to Mrs. Schlosser's uncle, and since his nine-year-old daughter was sleeping in the house at the time, this theory was quickly ruled out.

Another rumor was that the men who attacked Leona Schlosser may have been planning to rob homes in the area and that they set the fire in order to get the residents from their homes so that they could ransack the homes without being interrupted. But no valuables were touched in the Schlosser home, so this theory was ruled out as well.

The neighborhood was up in arms over this violent event. Neighbors began to raise funds to offer a reward for information that would lead to the arrest of the criminals. A bloodhound was even brought out to try to find the trail of the three assailants, but this came to naught.

Then on September 7, 1921, the *Watertown Daily Times* broke the news that three men had been arrested for the arson and assault on Leona Schlosser. The men were Henry Voss, a twenty-two-year-old divorced farmer; Frank Reuben Strop, thirty-three, a former serviceman who had been injured in World War I by a truck; and Herman Freitag, forty-five, a married man with a stepson. Each man, it was alleged, was a drinker, and Freitag was suspected of dealing in moonshine liquor.

The men were discovered by detectives of the Russell Detective Agency who had been brought in on the case to look for clues. They had been led to search a stone wall near the highway line fence. There, in a partially covered hole, they discovered two whiskey bottles that bore prescription labels from a Watertown doctor. The prescription had been filled by William Gehrke, a Watertown pharmacist. This, in turn, led detectives to arrest Henry Voss.

Voss seemed nervous and made so many contradictory statements that it led the detectives to think he was covering for someone. Voss was held in jail for half a day before he admitted his part in the Schlosser affair. He also named Strop and Freitag as accomplices. Voss went on to tell authorities that all three men had been drinking that night and that they decided to go over to the Schlosser home to have a little fun with Mrs. Schlosser. He went on to state that Freitag was the one who cut off her hair and later came back and doused the house in kerosene and set it ablaze. After the fire was set, the three men ran off.

When Strop was arrested, he made a similar confession, and both agreed that Freitag was the brains behind the entire affair. Freitag vehemently maintained his innocence. Ugly looks were exchanged between the three men while they were in court, and Strop and Voss looked to some as though they were a little worried.

Then on September 9, the *Times* announced that Voss and Strop had suddenly done an abrupt about-face and changed their confessions. Now they claimed that they had nothing to do with the arson or the attack on Leona Schlosser and that Herman Freitag had absolutely nothing to do with the crime as well. Voss and Strop claimed that their previous confession was the result of being given the "third degree" by the Russell Agency detectives.

Freitag was given a separate trial from the other two, and bail was set at $10,000 for each man. Only Freitag took advantage of this; the others preferred to wait out their time in jail. Enormous crowds surrounded the jail in Watertown's city hall on North First Street each day of the trial, and everyone had an opinion about the case.

The case was held over for the next term of the circuit court in February 1922. At that time, the first witness called was Leona Schlosser, who gave a recounting of her attack in a calm manner. Then came a reporter from a Jefferson newspaper, Adloh Adler, who testified that both Strop and Voss freely and without coercion had admitted their guilt.

Adolph Knaack was called next. He was Mrs. Schlosser's uncle, and he testified that on the night of the fire he was loading hay into his barn when he noticed his niece and nephew's house on fire. He didn't see anyone around who looked suspicious. He told the court how much of a settlement he got from the insurance company for the loss of his property due to the fire. Knaack also stated that the district attorney had asked him to go to Jefferson to try to get Voss and Strop to turn on Freitag, but they refused to turn against their cohort.

When Henry Voss was called to the stand, he continued to claim his innocence of the crime, claiming again that he and Strop had been beaten by the detectives into giving false confessions. On February 10, 1922, Herman Freitag was called to the witness stand. He claimed that he had gone to bed at 9:00 p.m. on the night of the crime and that he knew nothing about it all until the next morning, when he learned of the particulars from his neighbors. He also swore that he had not seen Strop or Voss for several months prior to the night in question.

The entire case, which was built mainly on circumstantial evidence at best, went to the jury on February 14, 1922. The lawyers made their final arguments, and at 9:30 a.m. the jury began its deliberations. Of the twelve empanelled, one juror was a woman, Mrs. Gertrude Wagner of nearby Fort Atkinson. By 11:30 a.m., the jury asked the judge to resend the charge of the court. By 10:00 p.m., the foreman of the jury, Mrs. Wagner, informed the court that they were hopelessly deadlocked. Mrs. Wagner later reported that she voted for conviction at each vote, but her vote was never enough to sway the other jurors.

Voss and Strop's case was held over until the September term of court, and they remained in jail until then. In September, when the case came up again, their lawyer asked to be excused because he was too ill to continue, so the case was held over until February 1923. Again there was a delay. It wasn't until October 1923, over two years after the whole affair, that the charges against the three defendants were finally dismissed due to insufficient evidence and they were released.

Thus, one of the most celebrated arson cases in Jefferson County came to an inglorious end. No one was found guilty and no one was held accountable for the attack on Leona Schlosser. All that remained were questions and more questions.

Chapter 5

WHAT GOES ON BEHIND
CLOSED DOORS

Families. They are either happy or they aren't. Fortunately, most are. They get along and live uneventful lives. But since these types of families don't make for interesting reading, we will dispense with them and zero in on the dysfunctional ones. There have been many dysfunctional ones in the history of Watertown. The stories that follow have little in common, except perhaps the presence of drinking and the acts of violence. These days, one tends to forget that cases of divorce, spousal abuse, child abuse and rape were as common in the nineteenth century as they are now. And these stories, coming from a period we all tend to romanticize, have the power to shock and disturb us.

We begin with the Gamble affair. On October 16, 1862, a murder took place three miles south of Watertown, not far from the scene of the Schlosser arson case discussed in the previous chapter. Michael Gamble, forty-two, while intoxicated, shot his wife, the former Mary Beggan. But how had things gotten to this point?

Michael Gamble was born in Ireland in 1820. He had immigrated to the United States with his brother and his wife, John and Margaret (Beggan) Gamble. The Beggans and Gambles bought land near each other in the town of Watertown and commenced farming. By 1845, John had acquired 120 acres of land, and Michael at this time had 40 acres, a yoke of cattle and two cows. The brothers were doing quite well for themselves in the New

World. On July 12, 1846, Michael married his brother's wife's sister, Mary, at St. Bernard's Catholic Church in Watertown. In 1848, Mary gave birth to a son whom they christened Michael Jr.

Michael Gamble was an industrious man, and his farm prospered. But he did have an unfortunate tendency toward strong drink, whiskey being his favorite libation. When he was under the influence, he could be hard to handle.

Tragedy struck the Gamble family in 1858. In that year, both John Gamble and his wife died, leaving behind them seven orphaned children. No one in the family had room for them, except Michael and Mary, who had only one child. So Michael and Mary became the guardians of the seven children. This created an enormous workload for Mary, and as for Michael, he began to turn more and more toward the bottle for relief and solace from his troubles. So the newly enlarged family struggled to make ends meet and get along. Then came the fatal day. Michael had gone into Watertown on some business and left his wife alone with a house full of children. After completing his business, Michael visited several saloons, and by the time he got back home, about 3:30 p.m. or so, he was quite drunk. Mary had gotten behind on her housekeeping and had not yet begun preparing the supper.

Drunk and hungry, Michael staggered into the room and plopped down on a chair by the table. He angrily demanded his evening meal. His wife, her nerves frayed by the children and other cares, shooed away the children and began to yell at her husband. He yelled back at her, and to punctuate his remarks, he began to throw dishes. Crockery soon began to fly about the room as Mary also started to throw dishes at her drink-sodden spouse. Even the children were caught in the crossfire as one was struck by the coffeepot as he tried to escape from the line of fire.

Mary got her final point across by throwing a teacup at her husband, which hit him near his left eye. Michael, who up to this point had been content with merely destroying the family's china, now picked up a chair and threw it against the wall. Fearing for her safety, Mary ran into the couple's bedroom and shut the door. She braced herself against it to prevent her husband from entering.

Catherine Gamble, one of the adopted children, was in the bedroom when her aunt came racing in. She helped her Aunt Mary to hold the door closed. Unable to pry the door open, Michael became more enraged. It was then that he noticed a shotgun standing nearby. A *loaded* shotgun. He picked it up and aimed at the bedroom door, firing point-blank at it. The shot went right through the door and entered into the left side of his wife, who was still standing against the other side.

Mary slumped down and asked her niece to help get her to safety. She asked to be taken down to the storm cellar, the opening of which was in the floor of the bedroom. Young Catherine slowly and with great difficulty helped her aunt get down into the cellar. Once her aunt was safe, Catherine made her escape by climbing out of a window and running for help. She ran to the home of their nearest neighbors, Mr. and Mrs. Timothy Daily.

While this was going on, Michael was busy reloading the shotgun and screaming threats. He now intended to shoot the entire family. But in his drunken state, he was unable to get the gun loaded properly, so he threw it down in disgust and ran out of the house. He was later found in the nearby orchard.

Neighbor Daily made his way over to the Gamble house and found Mrs. Gamble sitting in the cellar where Catherine had left her. He tried unsuccessfully to raise her up, but she was too heavy and weak from loss of blood. By the time Daily got her out of the cellar and placed her on the bed, she had died.

Michael Gamble was arrested and held in jail to await his trial, which began on February 24, 1863. It lasted but one day. The jury found him guilty of murder in the second degree, and he was sentenced to life imprisonment. The various children were parceled off amongst the relatives. Michael Jr. was sent to live with his uncle, Peter Gamble, a farmer who lived in nearby Ixonia. In the early 1870s, Michael Jr. moved to Minnesota, where he later married and in time became the father of six children.

In the meantime, Michael Gamble Sr. was not letting the grass grow under his feet. Now completely sober, he began, from his prison cell, to sell off his farm piece by piece in order to raise the money needed to finance an appeal. He was ultimately given a pardon by Governor Lucius Fairchild in 1869, but that was not without controversy. It was alleged that the governor was bribed in order to get him to sign the pardon. Governor Fairchild, however, steadfastly refuted this allegation. It was ultimately determined that Gamble had committed the murder while under the influence of alcohol and that, when sober, he was a harmless and inoffensive individual.

The pardon alleged that Gamble did not know that the gun was loaded or where his wife was standing when he shot through panels of the closed door. It was felt that Gamble had suffered enough and it was time for him to be released from prison. After he was freed, Michael left the area and joined his son in Minnesota. There he became a successful farmer and later even remarried. Michael Gamble died at the home of his son in 1912 at the age of ninety-two.

In the early 1870s, the murderous affairs of yet another dysfunctional family were revealed to the public. This murder actually took place not far from the Gamble farm in the town of Watertown. It occurred on November 30, 1874. John Borchardt, age about sixty-six, lived on a farm in the southeastern part of the township. With him lived his wife, Caroline, age fifty-one, and his two stepdaughters, Johanna (Hannah) and Wilhelmine (Mina) Krueger. He was described by those who knew him as friendly and without any enemies.

But obviously *someone* didn't like him!

About 8:00 p.m. on the night in question, Hannah and Mina Krueger, breathless and in an agitated state, arrived at the home of a neighbor, Rudolph Hoof, and told him that he must come quickly because someone had come into their house, doused the lights and struck their stepfather, wounding him badly. Hoof immediately set out with the girls to their home. As they went, the girls elaborated on their story, telling Hoof that their father had come home that night singing loudly as he entered the house. He greeted them all as he took off his things and asked his daughters to go out and tend to his horses.

While the girls were thus engaged, an unknown man came into the house, doused the lights, struck the old man and then ran off into the darkness. Hoof found this story to be a strange tale, made even stranger when the three met Caroline Borchardt standing outside of the house as they arrived. Mrs. Borchardt informed Hoof of her husband's death and told him that he had been kicked by a horse. It wasn't until her daughter Mina reminded her of the unknown assailant that Mrs. Borchardt changed her story to conform with her daughter's version.

Mr. Hoof began to feel very uneasy by this time, and he refused to enter the house. Instead, he went off to fetch another neighbor. However, this neighbor was equally bothered by the event, and he suggested that he and Hoof go after *another* neighbor. It was not until a brigade of eight men were assembled that anyone dared to enter the house.

Upon entering, the men found the three women in their nightclothes and huddled in bed together. There was a dim light in the room, and the men could just make out a form lying in the other bed. Upon closer inspection, it was revealed that this was the lifeless body of John Borchardt, his bloodied face covered by a cloth. The women seemed strangely unaffected by this gruesome sight. It was later reported that the women themselves had, in fact, carried the body and laid it upon the bed.

The men looked over the room. There was a large spot of blood on the floor, as well as on the lounge where the old man had been sitting when he was struck. The blood got on the floor, one of the women explained, when the old man fell and they dragged his body to the bed.

Questions began to be asked, but all of the women steadfastly maintained that a tall, dark man wearing a mask breezed into the house, blew out the lights and struck the old man. The blows John Borchardt received, as they were later described at the coroner's inquest by Dr. W.C. Spaulding of Watertown, were massive. There was a fracture at the base of the nose and five wounds to the scalp, four of which were broken through the skin to the bone. One wound had broken through the bone near the top of the head. There were several other wounds, some of which had broken through the bone, on the base of the skull and sides of the head near the ears. When the skull was opened, it was discovered that the deceased had suffered from massive internal bleeding as well.

In front of witnesses Wilhelmine stated that just before the old man expired he had said to her, "Mina, did you strike me?" This was a very surprising thing for her to have admitted, and it ultimately led to her downfall. The women were charged with murder and arrested. They still continued to assert their innocence. In the meantime, witnesses were examined, and from their testimony a very dark picture began to be painted of the Borchardt family.

The facts that came out at the trial, which lasted a mere two days, revealed that the old man and his family were not on good terms. He was quarrelsome and abusive, once even chasing his wife out of the house in the dead of winter. He scolded his wife on the night of his death. Borchardt was a heavy drinker, and even his own blood kin, his son Charles, had little use for him. When the girls came to Charles on the night of the murder, they asked him to fetch a doctor. Charles asked them if the old man wasn't actually drunk and merely being troublesome, which is why he didn't come over right away.

There was bad blood between the father and his stepdaughters as well, especially with Wilhelmine. The girls often talked about hiring themselves out for domestic work rather than live with the old man. It appears that John may have tried to kick Wilhelmine out of the house at one point, but this fact never was made clear, and at her trial, Wihelmine maintained that her stepfather always wanted her near him.

Perhaps the most damaging piece of evidence to come out at the trial was the report of a statement that Wilhelmine made to a friend. She was quoted as threatening that if her stepfather ever again chased her mother out of the house and locked her out to freeze she would "smash his head in."

But how did John Borchardt meet his death? No one ever found any tracks of this unknown assailant. Still, it could be argued that it snowed the night of the murder and the tracks, if they existed, were obliterated. Furthermore, Wilhelmine stated she saw the masked man run off toward Watertown, but no one else saw this phantom.

Then there was the means of death. John Borchardt was killed by blows delivered by a blunt instrument. When the premises were searched on the night of the murder, a bloody hammer was discovered in a cupboard. It was wrapped in clothes that had belonged to the deceased. None of the women remembered having seen the hammer in the house before the murder, though at the trial it was revealed by one of the daughters that their mother had asked Mr. Borchardt to bring her the hammer and some nails from the barn so that she could hang some curtains in the house.

The other telling feature of this case was the demeanor of the women. When the men entered the house, they found them in bed, laughing and talking animatedly. One of the daughters, Johanna, upon seeing the men enter, blurted out, "I did not harm him!" They also noted that the women seemed to whisper among themselves a great deal. They reportedly tried, unsuccessfully, to wash up the blood. And why did they feel it was necessary to move the body?

There also seems to be some evidence to believe that Johanna may have been suspicious of her mother and sister. While in prison, Wilhelmine wrote a threatening note to her sister that accused Johanna of always going against Wilhelmine and their mother. She concluded her note by threatening that "if you persist in doing so, mother will tell the whole story. You know a stranger came in and struck the old man; that we had nothing to do with it."

These questions all plagued the jury, but nevertheless, after deliberating for two hours they were able to render a verdict. In this case they found Caroline Borchardt and her daughter Wilhelmine Krueger guilty of murder. They were sentenced to life imprisonment at hard labor at the State Prison at Waupun, the first day of each year to be spent in solitary confinement. Johanna Krueger was cleared of all charges.

Incredibly, the two women were granted a pardon by the governor on September 22, 1880, on the grounds that the offense *was not murder* and that the punishment was already sufficient. The women returned to their home in the town of Watertown and, presumably, lived out their lives peacefully in sweet anonymity.

Not all dysfunctional family problems lead to murder. Sometimes they manifest themselves in other, heinous, ways. Terrible things, such as those that emerge in the story of the Karge family, happen behind closed doors and curtained windows.

The family seems to have moved around a bit, never staying in one place for too long. At the time of the incident, they were living in the northern part of Watertown, along Spaulding Street. Mr. and Mrs. Karge had been married in 1891 and were the parents of seven children. As Mr. Karge worked menial jobs, there wasn't much money, so times were hard for the struggling family.

Fred Karge turned to the solace of the bottle when things got too much to bear. He treated his wife brutally almost from their wedding day, yet she put up with this abusive treatment. He treated his children even worse. One daughter had been sent to the State Hospital in Winnebago, and the reason she was there was rumored to have been something her father had done to her.

And then there was the event that led up to the fateful day. Spaulding Street is normally a reasonably quiet street. It is rumored that Silver Creek, a tributary of the Rock River that flows through the area, is home to the storks that bring the babies. A quaint story. But there was no quaintness about the story that was unfolding in the Karge home. It seems that Fred Karge, tiring of his wife, had turned his attentions to his fifteen-year-old daughter, who was living at home, and he began to have relations with her.

Things came to a head on August 11, 1907, when Mrs. Ernestine Karge came running out of her house, latched on to patrolman Lucius Bruegger and begged him to come back to her house and arrest her husband. Hysterical, she informed him that her husband had beaten her and that then he had admitted that he had raped their daughter. Aghast, the officer was led back to the humble home, where he found Fred Karge, a tough-looking individual, sullenly sitting in the main room. In one corner was a shotgun, and it was later reported that Karge had threatened to kill anyone who came into the house. But he made no attempt to go for the gun when the officer came in. And in fact he put up no resistance whatsoever when he was arrested.

While in jail he said very little. He denied ever raping his daughter, and as for the other daughter in the state hospital, he would grow very violent if that was even mentioned. Karge's fifteen-year-old daughter was interviewed by the authorities, and she reported that her father had attempted to rape her once before and that he had only succeeded this time because he threatened to beat her.

Karge was hauled before the local justice of the peace and found guilty of assault and battery. He was fined ten dollars and court costs and, in default of this payment, was given a sentence of thirty days in the Dodge County jail in nearby Juneau. Once this term was up, he was then to have been arrested for the incest charge, according to the *Watertown Daily Times*.

In November 1907, Karge, still in jail awaiting his trial for incest, forced the bars out of his window and, using his blanket as rope, tried to escape from jail. Unfortunately, the rope blanket was "considerably too short." Since his cell was on the third story of the jail, he had a drop of several feet to the ground. He landed wrong and sustained a fracture of the leg and received a nasty cut to the face. The *Watertown Gazette* takes up the story: "After going a short distance, he [Karge] was forced to return, arriving at the jail shortly after a search for him had begun…It is a marvel that the man was able to walk at all with his leg in the condition that it was in when he returned to the jail."

Karge ultimately pleaded guilty to the incest charge, and he was sentenced to three years of hard labor at the State Prison at Waupun beginning on February 13, 1908. In 1911, he and his wife, Ernestine, were granted a divorce, and Mrs. Karge received custody of the children. She continued to move around and finally settled in the town of Ixonia. Her husband, meanwhile, appears to have passed away by 1917.

But this was not the end of the Karge family's suffering. Growing up in a dysfunctional family such as this one surely was, how could the children not be affected in some way? Such was the case with Fred Karge's son, Richard. In 1927, twenty years after the incest charge was first made, Richard Karge made the front page of the *Watertown Daily Times* when it was reported that he had killed a young woman in Milwaukee named Florence Sprecher by shooting her with a .22-caliber rifle. He then sat with her corpse for a while before taking his own life. They had seemed to be a happy couple, and young Karge was determined to marry his sweetheart. What drove him to this unhappy end is unknown, but Milwaukee police officials determined that this appeared to have been a suicide pact.

So ended yet another sad chapter in a Watertown family's life.

Chapter 6

ROBBERS, RASCALS AND RUFFIANS

The city of Watertown has always had more than its fair share of lawbreakers, rascals, robbers and ruffians. No doubt every comparably sized city in the United States has had the same. From Watertown's start, there has been that element who would do anything it takes to cheat, swindle or steal something from somebody else. However, these criminal types were the exception and not the norm. Most thievery was committed by a single person and relegated to a single event. With a few exceptions, they were usually caught and brought to justice. But by the 1850s, Watertown was experiencing a sudden rise in fortune. The railroad came through in 1855, and with it came immigrants, new settlers, new businesses and a new breed of lawbreaker: the career criminal.

The first career criminal to make his mark on the city was a sixteen-year-old hoodlum named Michael Dunlavy. He began his career in McHenry, Illinois, where he had been arrested for stealing forty dollars and a gold watch from the Western Hotel there. Dunlavy was not a very good robber and was caught red-handed in Illinois. But what he lacked in robbing skills he more than made up for in escaping skills, for as he was being held for trial he was able to escape from jail and make his way up to Wisconsin.

Once here, Dunlavy decided to pick up where he left off and began once again to rob hotels. The first hotel he picked was the Watertown House, located on the corner of South First and Market Streets. It was being run,

NEW COMMERCIAL HOTEL, 1886. Formerly known as the Watertown House, this was one of several hotels robbed by Michael Dunlavy in 1851.

at this time, by Joseph Lindon, who had been recently accused of horse stealing. Lindon would go on to become mayor of the city in 1863.

Dunlavy crept into the hotel around 11:00 p.m. on August 10, 1851. Before he entered the hotel, he had removed his hat and taken off his boots so as not to make any noise. Once inside, he tried several doors but found them all locked. Finally, he found one that was open, and upon entering he came face to face with Mrs. Lindon. She awoke with a start and demanded to know what the boy was doing there. Dunlavy, no doubt stunned for a second, bolted for the door and made good his escape. However, he left his hat and boots behind.

He hid out and regained his composure and decided to continue his crime spree. The next hotel he picked was the Watertown Exchange, the pioneer hotel in the city, run by Jacob Bell Van Alstine. About 2:00 a.m., he broke into the hotel, which sat on the corner of Main and North First Streets. Again he repeated his modus operandi of checking rooms until he found himself in the landlord's bedroom, which was located in the rear of the hotel.

Taking care not to wake the landlord, Dunlavy made off with Van Alstine's pants, which contained his wallet. Dunlavy took the wallet and left the pants in the dining room of the hotel. He then carefully went through the wallet, discarding what he thought was of no value, and in the end he pocketed about sixty dollars in cash. Not bad for ninety minutes' work. He then made his way out of the hotel through an open window.

The young felon might have gotten away had it not been for the fact that he felt it necessary to go back to the Watertown House to retrieve his hat and boots. While Dunlavy was engaged in robbing the Watertown Exchange, the Lindons down the street had placed a guard to watch for the return of the thief, and as Dunlavy came back for his property, he was caught. They held him in the barroom of the hotel until the constables could come and properly arrest him. While he was being held, the boy began to spin a yarn about being the unwilling pawn of two other accomplices, one named Reynolds and another man whom he described as "being rather tall, and had on…a light colored linen coat, satin vest, stripped or cross barred pants, the checks about an inch square, calicoe shirt, with fine dark figure, short whiskers and leghorn or palm leaf hat."

A portion of the stolen money was found on the boy, but he maintained that this was just his share and that the bulk of the money was held by the other two men. In due course the man named Reynolds was arrested, as was another man who matched the boy's description. They were both thoroughly searched, and no money was found.

Edwin B. Quiner, editor of the local Watertown newspaper the *Democratic State Register* (and great-uncle of future author Laura Ingalls Wilder), wrote of the case that Dunlavy "made so many statements…it is hard getting at the truth of the matter."

At the trial, Reynolds was examined and released, which created quite a public outcry in Watertown. Quiner editorialized in the pages of his paper that "the readiness with which villains escape unpunished in our community has induced rogues to make Watertown an especial point of operations." It is assumed that Dunlavy was sent away for his crimes, though there is no record of his ultimate fate.

About the same time that Dunlavy was trying to start a career robbing hotels, another youthful criminal was causing quite a stir in Watertown with a string of robberies. The boy's name was Habernich, and he was about seventeen years old. His career began on July 20, 1851, when he broke into a store owned by L.J. Fribert. The crime was committed sometime between 9:00 a.m. and 10:00 p.m. The clerks had been gone all day, and when they returned at 10:00 p.m. the crime was discovered.

The thief had gotten into the store via a cellar window. Once he came up the stairs, he used an auger to bore through the shop door and removed a crowbar that held the door in place. He proceeded to rifle through a desk and stole about forty-seven dollars. He then replaced the crowbar and made good his escape. He also robbed the American House, the Planters Hotel, the post office and the Dutch Store before leaving town. At each spot, he only came away with a small sum of money.

But young Habernich would meet his fate in the nearby city of Oconomowoc. There, on September 7, 1851, the store of a Mr. Collins was robbed of seventy dollars. Suspicion was aroused against the young man, who was seen heading toward Watertown after the robbery. The sheriff and a few Watertown citizens caught Habernich at a house about a mile east of Watertown. He was examined by the court in Waukesha County, and it was discovered that they were dealing with a very organized thief. He kept a very neat little account book of all the places he had robbed and the amounts he had come away with. Thus ended the career of someone who might be called Watertown's first "serial robber."

There were other robbers and other robberies, of course. Most were run of the mill, but some were remarkably brazen, such as the fellow who tried to rob the home of Mr. and Mrs. E. Levy on Second Street. On the night of June 3, 1878, a thief broke into the Levy home and began to ransack the place while the family was asleep upstairs. The robber made so much noise that it roused Mr. Levy from his slumber. Grabbing a pistol, Mr. Levy carefully came downstairs to investigate and confronted the robber in the act. A fight ensued, and the burglar shot at Levy and missed. Levy then shot at the burglar, but his gun jammed, thus allowing the thief to escape.

The noise of the gunshot roused the neighbors, and they came running over to the Levy home to see what was happening. Outside the house, they encountered a man in shirt-sleeves. When asked, the man said he didn't know what had happened and followed the crowd into the Levy home, where they found Mr. Levy and his wife in the dining room. Mrs. Levy had come downstairs halfway through the struggle between her husband and the robber. As she looked up, she noticed the very man who had attacked her husband standing in the crowd. Together with a neighbor lady, she managed to seize the man, grab his gun and drive him from the house.

But surely the career criminal who takes the prize in Watertown's history (at least in the nineteenth century) would have to be the "notorious" Mike Tracey. Michael Tracey was born about 1859 in Watertown, and his parents are believed to have been Michael and Maria Lawlor Tracey, Irish immigrants. The family was poor and lived in the old Seventh Ward of the city, known colloquially as the "Bloody Seventh," due to the combative nature of the Irish settlers who made their homes there.

A note should be made at this point about the ethnic diversity of Watertown. The city was founded by Yankee, or Yorker, settlers who migrated west from New York State, Connecticut and Vermont. They were closely followed by Irish settlers, many arriving after the potato famine of 1845. The Irish tended to settle in the south and southwestern areas of the city. The Germans began to arrive in the 1840s, with peak immigration taking place in the 1850s. The Germans settled in the northern and northeastern section of the city.

Most Irish settlers, especially those who emigrated during the time of the potato famine, brought little money with them but a strong work ethic. The Germans, on the other hand, not only brought money with them (which was sorely needed in the city's early days) but also business know-how. They quickly began to establish new industries such as brewing, soap making, tanning, cigar making and coopering. The Germans quickly outnumbered the Irish settlers, but the Irish and English still held the upper hand for many years because they spoke a common language. However, by the mid-1850s, German residents began to hold public office, and from then on it was a (fairly) level playing field.

Other ethnic groups to settle in the city were the Bohemians, who settled in a neighborhood located on the east side of the city, and the Welsh, who settled on the west side and also around the nearby town of Ixonia to the east. All the various groups got along reasonably well, with the exception of the Irish and the Germans, who seemed to thrive on provoking each other, especially at celebrations and during dances. Fights were common, hence the name "Bloody Seventh Ward" for the many Irish fighters who resided there.

Michael Tracey Sr. worked for the local railroad as an engine wiper. His son would also periodically work for the railroad. Mike Jr. grew up as a typical Watertown boy. As a young man, he worked as a painter for the interior decorating firm of Straw & Murphy, and about 1883 he married Carrie Weigel, the daughter of Franco-German emigrants. They had a daughter, Mary, born a few years after the marriage.

Why Mike Tracey went bad is unknown, but perhaps it was because he developed an unfortunate love of strong drink. At any rate, he began his long and sordid career in 1884. At this time, he and a few of his buddies were out drinking, and as they were walking up Fourth Street they got to arguing. One thing led to another, and soon one of them pulled out a knife and began to threaten the others. One of the party was hacked so terribly that it seemed unlikely that he would recover, and another man received severe stab wounds on his neck and face. However, Tracey was discharged by the court on the grounds that there was no cause of action against him. His partner in crime, William McGraw, the knife wielder, was held in jail on a $400 bond. Mike Tracey was lucky this time. He wouldn't be so lucky again.

In February 1886, Mike Tracey made the news again. This time the night watchman caught him red-handed in the act of burglarizing a saloon

WILLIAM RATHKE SALOON, CIRCA 1890S. This image illustrates two vices that plagued many young men in Watertown: gambling and drinking. In this picture are (left to right) William Jones, Max Shebstadt, H. Krueger, unknown and William Rathke. The saloon is now part of the *Watertown Daily Times* building. *Courtesy of Watertown Historical Society.*

owned by James Gingles on West Main Street. Well, perhaps *burglarizing* isn't quite the right description, since he was discovered drunk and hiding in the saloon's icebox! The items stolen were three boxes of sardines, some cigars, a bottle of ginger ale and about seventy cents in cash.

When apprehended, Tracey squealed on his accomplices, Pat Burke and James O'Malley. Burke, alias "George English," was later caught at O'Malley's home, where he had been whooping it up with liquor stolen from the saloon. O'Malley was let off, but Burke and Tracey were charged. Each served a jail term. Burke, it turned out, was a career criminal in his own right, having previously served twenty-one years in prison at Waupun. He boasted to a local newspaper reporter that his first offense had been for stealing and then he got sent away for fourteen years for being associated with a murder. He then was sent up for two years for another robbery and was finally given one year for grand larceny. In 1889, he was released from jail only to be nabbed again for being on "a straight drunk" and sentenced to five days in jail.

For his part in the robbery of the Gingles saloon, Tracey received one year at hard labor. Upon his release, he seems to have kept his nose clean and didn't make the papers again until 1889, when he was again arrested. This time he was pinched for stealing a watch from a student at Northwestern College in Watertown. Shortly thereafter, he was arrested again for public drunkenness. He tried to get out of jail time for this offense by telling the authorities that he was being held unjustly, since he already had a jail sentence to fulfill for the watch theft. Well, you can't argue with logic like that!

In 1891, "the notorious Mike Tracey," as he was being known, made the papers again when it was reported that he had been arrested for committing highway robbery. It seems that he robbed one Patrick O'Neil of twenty dollars near the South Third Street railroad crossing. He was arrested and sentenced to a term in the county jail. As the *Watertown Republican* reported at the time, "Tracey seems to court notoriety and is never easy until he commits some misdeed that gets him behind bars."

The "notorious Mike Tracey" made the news one last time in 1904 when he was arrested in Janesville for petty larceny. He was sentenced to six months in Waupun for his crime. Mike Tracey died a pauper in 1905. His wife, Carrie, meanwhile, had gone into the millinery business and ran a successful dress-making establishment until her death from cancer in 1918.

Lest it be thought that only men could be thugs, we present the story of Maggie O'Connell. She was an 1880s phenomenon who sprang into the news in 1881 and all but disappeared by 1889. But during the years when she was engaged in her criminal pursuit, the press had a field day.

Her like had never been seen before in Watertown. The only other woman to come close to touching her in terms of sheer brazenness was the "notorious" Mrs. Brandt, who, in the 1870s, made headlines by stealing a cow and hiding out with it. She was later caught when she came back to Watertown to visit her sick mother.

There was also Ellen McDermott, known scornfully as "Crazy Nellie." She lived in the vicinity of North Monroe Street on the city's west side. Ellen was not a thug but more a pitiful creature with odd quirks. She lived alone in a rude little shanty in abject poverty. The area children taunted her. She was treated rather badly. But Ellen was a proud woman, and in order to make ends meet she took in washing. She also kept a garden, and here is where one of her most colorful personality traits manifested itself. It seems that she was known to swear loudly and profanely at the insects that infested her plantings. This sort of behavior did not win her many supporters. However, the editor of the *Watertown Democrat*, Daniel Ballou, rose to her defense and scolded children and others who bothered Ellen. Ballou also urged the city fathers to build her a proper home, but they never did. She disappears from history in the late 1870s.

But Maggie O'Connell was unique. Truth be told, the most outrageous of her exploits took place in Illinois, not in Watertown. But news of her latest exploits always made their way back to her hometown, and oh, did she make Watertown proud!

She was born Margaret O'Malley. Her brother, James, was the same man who was in cahoots with the "notorious" Mike Tracey in the Gingles saloon robbery in 1886. James was no prize, and he spent time in jail, once even serving a sentence along with his sister. His crime was stealing. Hers was being drunk and disorderly.

Maggie was apparently married at some point, but the details are not known, since she seems to have also gone by several aliases, Crowley and Miller being the most frequent ones. According to an 1883 newspaper article, she claimed that she was twenty-six years old and the mother of two. She went on to state that she had married her husband, presumably Mr. O'Connell, at the age of fifteen and that he had started her down the road to ruin. She claimed that she was unhappy with the marriage and had left her husband and, it is to be assumed, her children as well, for this is the only mention of them ever.

She first made the news in 1881 when she was serving time in jail in Janesville, a city in south central Wisconsin near the Wisconsin-Illinois border. While there, she attempted suicide, but she managed to cheat death and was, according to a contemporary newspaper account, working in the kitchen of the Madison Asylum. Jail time and frequent suicide attempts are a running theme in the story of Maggie O'Connell, as is drinking.

In 1883, Maggie was in Chicago in an insane asylum. This time, she told reporters that she was being held there against her will. The authorities maintained that she was picked up for being drunk and losing her reason as a result. Her aged father in Watertown wrote a pathetic letter of appeal, asking the powers-that-be to release his daughter and send her back home to her family. After due deliberation, she was sent home to Watertown once more.

In 1884, she reappears in the Watertown papers, where she is described as being "dissolute and wretched in appearance." She was beginning to be referred to in print as "the wayward and unfortunate female, Maggie O'Connell." This time, she was arrested for stealing a pair of shoes from local shoemaker Friedrich Pohlmann and sentenced to thirty days in jail. While in the hoosegow, she made life miserable for her fellow inmates by yelling continuously for water. Yet when it was brought to her, she would refuse to drink it and pour the contents on the floor. A newspaper contemptuously reported that she was probably hoping for whiskey.

Later in 1884, while serving a jail term in Jefferson, she again attempted suicide by hanging herself, only to once more cheat death when the sheriff found her in the nick of time and was able to revive her. After her release, Maggie left Watertown and headed for Milwaukee, where she was promptly arrested for breaking and entering. She returned to Watertown once more, just in time to be arrested once again for theft, and then she fled the state, winding up in Rockford, Illinois.

Using the alias Maggie Miller, she committed a string of petty thefts in Rockford, and when caught, she proudly boasted to the officers that she had been in jail in Oregon, Dixon and Freeport just recently for similar offenses. The newspaper account of her arrest ended with this juicy bit of Maggie O'Connell panache: "She was held on $100.00 bonds to the grand jury, and rode through the streets in the patrol wagon singing a ribald song at the top of her lungs." What a way to go!

Shortly after her incarceration, she once again attempted suicide by hanging herself in her cell, only to be saved once again by the quick action of a well-meaning sheriff who cut her down in the nick of time.

She must have found Illinois a more congenial place to live, for she seems to have spent the next few years visiting every jail in the state. In 1887, she again made the Watertown papers when she turned up in Chicago. Maggie was in jail again and was described as "making the welkin ring with her yells" while in custody. Her offense was once more petty theft, and the authorities sent her to the asylum in Kankakee, Illinois. While in the asylum, Maggie claimed that she was mentally disturbed due to her terrible experiences in the famous Newhall House fire in Milwaukee. When the Watertown press got wind of this claim, it remarked, "Long before that she developed many of her wicked freaks."

Shortly thereafter, she returned once more to Watertown, and in late 1887, she was once more arrested for theft. This time she had been caught going from house to house on South Third Street begging for food. She carried with her a piece of beef wrapped in old clothes. She was apparently trying to pass it off as an infant. At one house, she managed to break in and make off with a satchel that contained a small sum of money. She made her way over to a nearby saloon, where she bought some tobacco, rolling papers, matches and whiskey. She was caught soon after and sentenced to one year at hard labor in prison.

She all but disappears from history after that, save for a letter on file with the Jefferson County Court dated 1905 in which the then–district attorney, Joseph E. Davies (later ambassador to Russia), petitioned the court to have her committed to the State Asylum in Mendota, where, it is assumed, she died.

Chapter 7

LOVE IS A
MANY-SPLENDORED THING

Love. What a powerful emotion. It can make even the most ordinary person do extraordinary things. Take the case of the young woman in Watertown in the 1870s who wanted to have a photograph taken of herself to give to her sweetheart. She went into one popular photo studio and made inquiries, and the photographer explained the different poses he could take. They were full figure, bust or knee position. After carefully pondering the matter, the young woman stated that she would like to have a bust shot but asked the photographer to please get her head in the picture as well.

After she got her picture, she presented it with due ceremony to her beau the very next time they kept company together. Her Romeo was overjoyed with the likeness, and after carefully wrapping it in a handkerchief, he promised her that he would always keep her picture close to his heart. However, the next time they got together, her lover felt a sneeze coming on, and reaching into his back trouser pocket, he pulled out a hankie to suffuse the blow. In doing so, the picture of the young man's intended fell out. The young woman got very offended by this and went around telling everyone that obviously her man's "heart was not in the right place."

A more tragic story revolving around the theme of love is the Kellermann case. On October 28, 1899, at 4:30 a.m., Louis Kellermann, twenty-eight, a former well driller in Watertown, made his way over to his father-in-law's house on the east side of the city near Northwestern College. Once there, he removed his shoes and crawled through the basement window. He made his way up to a bedroom where his estranged wife, Lizzie, and her sister were sleeping.

His wife's sister, Emilie, awoke, and placing her feet on the floor, she accidentally stepped on Louis, who was on his hands and knees at the time. Before either woman could cry out, Louis jumped up and shot his wife with a .22-caliber revolver. The bullet entered Lizzie Kellermann's cheek and lodged in the base of her brain.

After the shooting, Louis fled the scene. He finally came to rest in the hayloft of his mother's barn. There, on October 29, 1899, about 6:30 p.m., Louis Kellermann took the same gun that he had shot his wife with and shot himself. His body was discovered by his younger brother, who was investigating a sound he heard coming from the barn.

The coroner's jury ruled his death a suicide. It was felt that he took his own life to atone for shooting his wife. As for Lizzie, she ultimately recovered from her wound. It later came out that Louis had made plans to move to Milwaukee, to start anew, and that he was hoping to induce his wife to come with him. But she had refused and left him to return to her father's home instead.

The heart is a cruel organ. It often makes people fall in love with the wrong sorts. For example, sometimes the objects of our affection are already involved with another. Love triangles are never easy and rarely lead to happiness. Someone always winds up being hurt—or worse. Take the story of Meta Tessman, a perfectly normal woman who was driven to a desperate act by love.

The former Meta Ladien was born in nearby Aztalan on December 15, 1886. In 1908, she married John Tessman, and the couple had seven children. Outwardly, the marriage seemed to be a happy one, but such was not the case. The family moved to Watertown and lived at several different addresses while John worked at several menial jobs. In 1927, the family was living in the northern part of the city, and John had secured a janitorial job. Meta, in order to make ends meet, had taken a job at the local shoe factory.

In March 1928, Meta left the shoe factory and went to work for John H. Deakin, the owner of a Blair Super Service on Third Street. Her job there was to keep the books and do general labor around the office. Things went along smoothly for a time. Then trouble began to appear. John Deakin had a very jealous wife. Elizabeth Deakin began to get suspicious about her husband's new employee, especially when Meta began to call the Deakin house at all hours and hang up whenever Elizabeth answered the phone.

Mrs. Deakin had heard unpleasant rumors about Meta, and she began to work on her husband, nagging him to fire Meta. Unable to deal with the unpleasantness at home, John Deakin finally bowed to his wife's wishes and discharged Meta Tessman in July. Meta did not take this with good grace. She called Mrs. Deakin all manner of filthy names and ended her tirade with a threat: "Revenge is sweet. I'll get you, you old SOB, yet!"

With Meta gone, things should have calmed down, but they did not. Meta kept on calling the Deakin house, asking to speak to John. About this time, she also tried to secure a divorce from her husband of twenty years, but the judge refused to hear the case and told them to patch up their differences for the children's sake. Thwarted, Meta simply left her husband and family and moved into a boardinghouse.

Meta now began to put in motion a plan to get rid of Elizabeth Deakin. On August 7, 1928, she went into the Charles Doerr drugstore on West Main Street and purchased thirty-five cents' worth of strychnine. She claimed that she was going to use it to kill rodents in her apartment. Once the method was in her hands, all she needed to do was to bide her time.

Her chance finally came on February 7, 1929. That day, Elizabeth Deakin went out to check the morning mail and found a package addressed to her. Inside were the remains of an Eskimo Pie ice cream bar that had partially melted. There was also a note that read: "Dear Mrs. Deakin: Was to see you but you were not at home. Have one on me. Will see you later. From—guess."

The handwriting looked vaguely familiar to Elizabeth. She took the parcel inside and asked her husband what she should do. He advised her to never eat anything that came through the mail, so Mrs. Deakin placed the parcel

718 MARKET STREET. This was the duplex occupied by Elizabeth Deakin and her husband in 1929 when an attempt was made to poison her. This home was razed in 1986 to make way for a fast-food restaurant. *Courtesy of Watertown Historical Society.*

in the pantry. Some of the melted ice cream had leaked on to her hand and she licked it off. The taste, she noted, seemed odd somehow.

At her husband's suggestion, she took the parcel to their family doctor, Dr. Willard Waite. He, in turn, sent the contents on to Dr. Clarence W. Muehlberger, a toxicologist at that time residing in Madison. He took several tests and discovered that the ice cream bar was laced with enough strychnine to kill several people. When informed of the news, Elizabeth Deakin immediately began to suspect Meta Tessman.

In addition to being a jealous woman, Mrs. Deakin was also a very intelligent woman, and she knew that she needed concrete evidence to convict Mrs. Tessman. She began by comparing the handwriting in the note to the entries Meta had made in her husband's books. Unfortunately, there wasn't enough to really compare with in the records, so she hatched a plan.

Elizabeth Deakin composed two letters addressed to Mrs. Tessman. In the letters, she pretended to be her husband. Meta took the bait, and on one day in November 1929, Elizabeth received morning and afternoon deliveries of letters from Meta. One letter, which was later entered into evidence at trial, read as follows:

Sweetheart, my dearest love. Just got your letter and sure was glad to hear from you. I have not heard anything more as yet but dear for God's sake don't let anyone see that your in town. They may not suspect anything rong this week but wait untill next. If you are not here then the fun will begain so please get everything you want to do OK this week so as to get away from here or you will have some fun. Now Sweetheart listen to me. Don't wait untill its too late. Please dear Darling dear I am just sick. I cannot stand any more. I want you to take me away from all this trouble. Please honey do. I love you. God only knows I do and how I cannot live without you. I just can't aney more dear so please don't make me suffer aney more and let's go before its too late and sweetheart—don't—believe the bad things thay tell you about me honey thay are not true... You'll know next week for sure. I am all sat. If you don't you will know when and why I done this terrible thing. The more I think about it the sicker it makes me feel. Let me know at once what you will do and I want you to tip toe through the two lips with me Sweetheart from your one true love with a million kisses to you only. M.

With the letters in hand, Elizabeth Deakin went to see John F. Tyrell, a handwriting expert in Milwaukee, who examined the letters and the note and concluded that the writing on all the documents was done by Meta

Tessman. Mrs. Deakin then went to the authorities and swore out a warrant against Mrs. Tessman for attempted murder.

In the meantime, both John Deakin and Meta Tessman had fled the scene. John's whereabouts were unknown for some time, but Meta was discovered living under the name Mrs. John Deakin in Chicago. She had been working as a cook at the Planters Hotel there. Elizabeth Deakin also left town to stay with relatives in Pardeeville, Wisconsin, for a time.

When informed of the charges, Meta declared them to be ridiculous and denied everything. The State of Wisconsin tried to have her extradited back to Jefferson County, but she managed to fight the order until February 1930, when she was finally returned to stand trial. She was held in jail on a $5,000 bond.

On May 10, 1930, the case took a dramatic turn when the press announced that Meta Tessman had escaped jail. In the early hours of the morning, she somehow managed to saw through the bars and make her escape. How she came by the saw is unknown, but the police went hunting for a Watertown woman who was suspected of being her accomplice.

On the same day she escaped, she was appended by Sheriff John C. Gruel, who was acting on a tip received from one of Meta's relatives, Paul Ladien. She had been hiding out in Ladien's house while she was waiting for a car to take her to Chicago. It was later revealed that two weeks prior to this attempt, she had made a previous escape from jail and that she had, in fact, actually made it all the way to Chicago, only to be met there by Sheriff Gruel and returned to her cell in Jefferson. She was charged with jailbreaking, which meant that if she was found guilty of the poisoning charge she would face an additional six months for the jailbreak.

On October 8, 1930, after being held in the Jefferson County jail since her escape attempt in May, Meta Tessman suddenly found herself free. Her case had been halted by the circuit court owing to Elizabeth Deakin's failure to appear and testify. Where was Mrs. Deakin? It appears that she had left her relatives in Pardeeville and traveled to Chicago to confront her husband. Mrs. Tessman also, upon release, boarded a train heading for Chicago. The Tessman poisoning case was formally dismissed in February 1931. At this time, all of the parties in the action were residing in Chicago.

Sometime later, Meta returned to Wisconsin and took up residence in Milwaukee. She died in 1939 in an auto crash. John Deakin died in Chicago in 1952. Elizabeth Deakin returned to Pardeeville and died there in 1958, thus bringing down the final curtain on the Tessman poisoning case once and for all.

Love makes people do strange and irrational things, as these stories illustrate. In this next case, love plays only a minor role, but it was a factor.

This story involves a bachelor farmer of means and a drunken quarrel that led to murder. On October 3, 1936, at a handsome farm located along Highway 19 just west of the city limits, a murder took place. It seems that William Voss, age sixty, had beaten his neighbor, Ferdinand Engelke, age fifty-nine, to death.

Voss, a farmer, had been drinking heavily most of the day. He had visited the Leonard Oestreich farm earlier and demanded money. When he was refused, he cut across lots to the Engelke farm. Once there, he and Ferd had a few drinks in the barn. It seems that Ferd always kept a bottle in there just for this sort of an occasion. After a while, they adjourned to the house and drank some more in the kitchen.

They went into the living room, and while there, Voss noticed a picture of a woman hanging on the wall. It was a photo of Ferd's housekeeper. His *former* housekeeper. Voss made a crass remark about the woman in the picture, accusing Engelke of being her boyfriend. This seems to have struck a nerve with Engelke, and he took offense. Perhaps there was more to the relationship than just employer and employee?

WILLIAM VOSS. This posed shot of the murderer of Ferdinand Engelke was staged for a photographer from the local newspaper. *Courtesy of* Watertown Daily Times.

In any event, Ferd tore out of the room and got his shotgun. Voss, who was deaf, didn't hear him grab the gun, but when he returned to the kitchen and saw Ferd with it in his hand he figured he was about to be shot. To defend himself, Voss picked up a piece of firewood near the stove and advanced on Engelke, clubbing him over the head with the piece of wood. As Engelke fell, Voss made a grab for the shotgun and ran outside the house with it. Upon his return, he found that Ferd had wandered into the living room. Ferd was holding his head and bleeding from being struck.

Voss panicked. He believed that Engelke was going to get another gun, so he did the only thing he could think of. He got another piece of stove wood and proceeded to beat Ferdinand Engelke to death with it. This way, he reasoned, there would be no one around to tell the authorities who had committed the foul deed.

After Ferd was dead, Voss decided that he had to do away with the corpse, so he looked around for some kerosene with which to set the place ablaze. All he could find was some varnish. So he poured a ring of the fluid around the body, lit it and ran out. Unfortunately for him, the varnish did little more than smolder. The next morning, a neighbor, Fred Timm, came to

ENGELKE MURDER SCENE, 1936. The "X" marks the spot where the lifeless body of Ferdinand Engelke was discovered. *Courtesy of* Watertown Daily Times.

pick apples. When he noticed that Ferd wasn't out and about like he usually was, he went inside the house to investigate and found the body lying on the living room floor.

Voss, meanwhile, had left the Engelke farm and run to a farm one and a half miles west on Highway 19 belonging to Walter Mohr. There he crawled into the barn and slept for a while, leaving the Mohr farm about 4:00 a.m.

The police were somewhat baffled by the murder, as Engelke was apparently well liked. They began their investigations and soon got a break. A local tavern owner, Edward Demant, reported to the police that he had been serving William Voss. Voss had been talking about the murder, and he seemed to know too much. This made Demant suspicious, and he alerted the cops. Voss was arrested and taken to the city jail.

VOSS BEING LED TO JAIL. This photo shows William Voss (second from left) being led to his cell by (left to right) Officer Arthur Zimmermann, Harry O'Brien and Harold Dakin. *Courtesy of Mary Rohr.*

While there, he seemed sullen and depressed and told the authorities that he didn't much care what happened to him, as he was dying of a form of cancer, which later turned out to be untrue. He also tried, unsuccessfully, to commit suicide while in jail by cutting his wrists with a boot nail. He denied any knowledge of the crime at first, but gradually, through the prodding of Officer Harry O'Brien (a friend of his), he finally admitted to the whole affair, even returning to the crime scene to pose for pictures reenacting the crime. He was sentenced to fifteen years in prison at Waupun. In 1941, he tried to petition the governor for a pardon, but he was denied.

A spurned lover is the worst kind of enemy to have at times. Take the case of James W. Crawford. In 1854, he was jilted by a young woman. How did he react to this? Not well. In fact, he went straight to a Watertown printer's shop and asked the printer to produce a handbill in which he laid out, in no uncertain terms, the story of his former lover's infidelity. He also had a few choice things to stay about not only her character but also the character of the new man she was seeing.

The printer was a bit hesitant at first, but Crawford assured him that everything he wrote out was true. Pocketing a fee for the job, the printer went to work. In due course, several of these scandalous sheets went flying out of the press. Crawford had them distributed throughout Watertown and the countryside. The handbills made their first appearance on July 17, 1854. One of the scandal sheets found its way into the hands of the girl's father, J.E. Arnold of Milwaukee, who had been in Madison attending a session of the Supreme Court. Maligning the daughter of J.E. Arnold was not a smart thing to do, because he was a man of principle and had quite a temper, as Crawford was to find out in due course.

The irate father set out from Madison and headed straight to Watertown. He angrily questioned the printer and was told to seek out James Crawford. Arnold found him in the parlor of the Planters Hotel, which was located on the southeastern corner of Main and South First Streets. (Today a real estate agency is located on this site.)

Crawford pleaded innocence, but there were parts of his story that didn't seem to ring quite true. Ultimately, the girl's angry father pulled out a rawhide whip, intending to flog the villainous cad who had so egregiously insulted his daughter's character. He began to whip Crawford, and the two men struggled. Crawford ultimately managed to grab the whip from Arnold, and he began to whip his attacker.

This prompted Arnold to pull out a revolver. Crawford, like the craven coward that he was, took one look at the gun and bolted from the room,

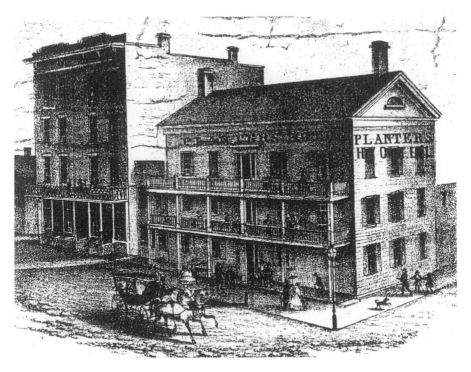

THE PLANTERS HOTEL, 1857. Here, in the parlor, is where J.E. Arnold attacked James Crawford for maligning his daughter's character in 1854. This building burned to the ground in 1869.

shutting the door behind him and holding it closed so that he could not be pursued. Realizing that this was only a temporary measure, Crawford ran out of the hotel and north up First Street, with an angry Arnold hot on his tail.

Arnold fired once, but the ball bounced off Crawford's boot heel. He fired again but this time missed. Crawford got a little bold now, realizing that his opponent was a punk shot, and he actually had the nerve to turn back and make an obscene gesture to the old man. Enraged, Arnold advanced again, and Crawford's bravado once more left him as he turned tail and ran. He ran for about thirty feet and then slipped and fell. Arnold shot at him and missed him again, but seeing Crawford lying on the street, he thought he had wounded him. His daughter's honor avenged, Arnold returned to the hotel, where he was later arrested for reckless endangerment and attempted murder. Crawford continued to plead innocence, but the tide of public opinion soon turned against him, and he left town.

Ah love—it's a many-splendored thing, isn't it?

Chapter 8
GHOSTLY ENCOUNTERS

From tales of real, flesh-and-blood human beings, we now turn to the supernatural. Just about every city and town has its own stories of hauntings and tales of unexplained phenomena, and Watertown is no exception. These stories are hard to prove, and many are somewhat unbelievable, but when we hear a noise in the night or feel a presence in a room when there is no one there, who is to say what is real?

We begin with the story of George Schinnick, a member of the Jefferson County Board from Watertown. One afternoon in the latter half of the nineteenth century when he was a young man, he was driving a wagon into the city to buy supplies. After he had finished his business in the city, he got back into his wagon and headed for home. His farm was on the River Road, which is southwest of the city. It was just dusk. The horse was going along at a gentle trot, and he was calmly and pensively holding the reins and watching the road ahead.

Suddenly, he began to break out in a cold sweat. Turning, he saw a man in a black suit sitting beside him. The man's coat collar was wrapped around his neck, and he was wearing a broad-rimmed hat. For several minutes, Schinnick, filled with fear, said nothing. Then, overcoming his feeling of dread, he mustered up the courage to ask the dark figure what he was doing there.

But the figure remained silent.

Schinnick asked again, and again he was met with silence. Finally, he grabbed the buggy whip and threatened to strike the man in black if he didn't tell him who he was and why he was there. Whereupon the figure vanished as suddenly as it had appeared. George drove on for another half a mile before once more the figure in black reappeared. Overwhelmed by fear, George yelled at the figure once more and once again grabbed the whip and attempted to strike when the figure disappeared as before.

George now whipped the horses up and drove as fast as he could to his home. Once there, he sat in the wagon and trembled with fear for a time, his nerves nearly wrecked. There was never any explanation given as to why this phenomenon occurred.

Ghosts are unpredictable. For a while in the latter half of the nineteenth century, there was a belief that a specter haunted the center of the North Second Street bridge, known in Watertown as "the Cow Bridge," and people in the area were filled with fear at the prospect of having to travel across the bridge at night. Though the specter hasn't been seen in years, there are those living in Watertown today who claim that one of the houses located on the south end of the bridge is haunted. It is said that strange lights have been seen coming from its windows. Who is to say it is not true?

Sometimes ghostly sightings are merely cases of misunderstanding. Take the story of the burly fellow who worked as an undertaker's assistant. One would think that, being constantly exposed to the trappings of funerals and preparations of deceased individuals, he would have been impervious to ghosts. But in January 1893, while he was fitting up a coffin for a departed friend, he got the fright of his life. It seems that while he was thus occupied, a young woman dressed in an outrageous costume wandered into the funeral parlor to check her makeup for a masquerade party to be held that night. He looked up from his labors, took one look at the young woman in her costume and thought one his clients had risen from the grave. On her part, the young woman, thinking that the place was empty, was startled by the man and let out an ear-splitting scream that almost drove him into hysterics! Both ran off, and it was, in the words of the newspaper report, "hard to tell which was the most scared of the two."

Watertown has a total of five cemeteries within its city boundaries. Each cemetery contains the mortal remains of former residents. They are beautiful places, in their own way. Cemeteries, for the most part, hold no real terror in Watertown. Oh, there were cases of strange happenings at night at Oak Hill Cemetery, one of the oldest cemeteries in the city and the final resting place for many of Watertown's pioneer settlers, but these were not ghostly in nature. They were merely the exchange of illegal moonshine liquor during the era of Prohibition. No, cemeteries never held real terror for Watertown citizens. But haunted houses, on the other hand, well, that's a different story.

Most cities have haunted homes; some even have built a whole tourism trade around them. In Watertown, there are a few, and it is more than likely that once this book is published more will surface. For example, on North Fourth Street in the northern part of the city, there is a house that was haunted by the ghost of a child who, supposedly, met her fate in some unexplained manner. No strange deaths have ever been attributed to the house, but locals insist this was the case, and one former resident of the home claimed that there was a walled-off area in the basement from which came the sounds of a child crying. There was also a sewing room on the first floor in which an unearthly force was felt that prevented people from occupying the room for too long.

Then there is a house along North Church Street that is haunted by the ghost of its original owner and builder. This ghost is, for the most part, friendly in nature and even allowed itself on one occasion to be "photographed." The image shows a wall painted with a dull finish, yet there is a flash of light on it that, the owners of the house are convinced, is the spirit.

Though technically not a true haunted house, the Old Faith Home on Margaret Street did have a very strange beginning, and many people at the time suspected the denizens of the place to have supernatural powers. Built in the late 1880s, the place was a sort of revivalist haven run by a "Reverend" Boswell who was known as "The Prophet." Many who came there were interested in faith healing and the psychic activities that may have been demonstrated and encouraged. People came from far and wide with disabilities, hoping for a cure. In the summer months, tents were pitched around the building to accommodate the overflow of customers, and strange goings-on took place, along with a considerable consumption of beer and other spirits. Later, it became a Christian Science headquarters, and then it became the Watertown Bible Institute. In 1904, it was rented out by a Lutheran KindeFreund Association as a "home for the feeble-minded," which later became Bethesda Lutheran Home, a nationally recognized care facility for the developmentally disabled. In the 1920s, a fire raged through the building, destroying the third story and its distinctive Moorish tower, and the remaining structure became an apartment building.

There were rumors of it being haunted as well. It was claimed that voices could be heard throughout the building, but it was later revealed that the walls were so thin that voices and other noises from the apartments could be heard all over the building. So much for spirits.

OLD FAITH HOME, CIRCA 1890S. Built in the late 1880s, this was the site of strange goings-on involving faith healing and other practices. It was also believed to have been haunted. *Courtesy of Watertown Historical Society.*

Perhaps the most famous haunted house in Watertown is the Cleveland Street poltergeist house. The house was built by local mason Christian Schmutzler soon after he arrived from Germany in 1851. He designed it to be a replica of his ancestral home in Bavaria. The home is of brick construction with a stucco covering made to look like stonework that had been beveled. Fluted pilasters at each corner of the house and elaborate entablatures beneath each window give the home a distinct classical look.

For years, no word of hauntings or any other strange goings-on was reported there. Then, in 1977, the home was rented by Mr. and Mrs. Charles Franta and their family, and they went through a series of very strange events that they concluded resulted from the house being possessed by a poltergeist.

The nightmare began for the family when they took up residence in the home. One night shortly after they moved in, Mr. Franta was away at work and his wife was at home watching TV. Suddenly, she felt a cold chill, but no windows were open. This happened five nights in a row. She later claimed that it felt like someone was standing right behind her.

On another occasion, one of their children was asleep when suddenly she awoke screaming. The whole household came running to see what was the

POLTERGEIST HOUSE. This image shows the infamous Cleveland Street haunted house. It is believed that it is possessed by an evil poltergeist.

matter, and through her tears the little girl told them that someone had been sitting on her bed, but no one was there. Two nights later, this same child was awakened by the sounds of scratching in her closet, but when her parents investigated, once again there was nothing there.

Then their son was climbing the stairs one day, and all of a sudden he let out a scream and came flying down the steps, landing on his face. It was claimed, after he was examined, that the boy hadn't fallen down the steps. He was pushed. There were even bruises that resembled finger marks found on the boy's waist, as if someone or something had grabbed him and thrown him.

Not long after that, the poltergeist struck again. When Charles went to place his son on a rocking horse, the toy began to rock furiously by itself. The child started screaming, and his father had to quickly pull him off the horse.

The terrified family had had enough, and they moved out after only staying in the home for three months. Not long after that, the family learned that there was a rumor that a murder had taken place in the house and that therefore the house possessed a restless spirit. There was no proof of a murder ever having taken place there and no reports of any paranormal activity since then. But even current renters report that they have experienced nothing but bad luck since moving into the house. Now, it should be noted that this story is definitely true, for it ran in the *National Enquirer*, and that pillar of the publishing world wouldn't run a lie, now would it?

We leave the realm of the supernatural and present a tale of demonic possession that took place in Watertown, the case of Carl Siege. It all began in the winter of 1869. A family of German immigrants had moved into a small house on the south end of South Fifth Street near the Milwaukee and St. Paul Railroad depot just two years before. They were poor, and some might call them shiftless. An example of this is the fact that they had applied to each church in the city for handouts, exhausting each charity in turn rather than work for their daily bread. The family was made up of parents, a daughter and her little infant and a son named Carl, who was about twenty-six years old at the time of the incident. Carl was partially paralyzed on his right side and had a twisted and withered right hand. He was also, in the words of the *Watertown Democrat*, "probably insane or idiotic."

While living in Germany, Carl would often have seizures in which he would smite his fists, foam at the mouth and shake the table until the food and plates would go flying. These fits came on him at unpredictable times and often lasted a day or more. These conditions only worsened after they arrived in America.

Once here, the family boarded out their daughter, a lass of sixteen, to the family of a local Lutheran minister. He took advantage of the girl and got her pregnant. He was later arrested for this, and while in jail he hanged himself. The girl came back to her family in disgrace and, not long after, gave birth to a child. This child became the object of Carl's fits from then on. He often tried to attack the baby and had to be restrained.

The family finally decided to seek some help for their son. They consulted with Dr. John Peter Quinney, the son of a Stockbridge Indian chief who had come to the city in 1861. He made his home at 500 Division Street, where he grew his herbs for his medical treatment. Dr. Quinney examined the boy and administered a strong herbal physic and applied drawing plasters to Carl's shoulders. When the plasters were removed the next day, they were found to be covered with small, multicolored worms or bristles. On another occasion, it was claimed that Carl had swallowed a snake and that the reptile was trying to climb out of his throat. Dr. Quinney threw in the towel, and the family came to the conclusion that medical science couldn't help their son. He needed the help of the church, for obviously he was possessed by the devil.

INTERIOR OF ST. HENRY'S CATHOLIC CHURCH, CIRCA 1873. It was on this church's altar, located in the center of the image, that the solemn rites of exorcism were performed on Carl Siege in 1869.

The family turned to a Catholic priest for help, but since they were Protestants the priest refused to help them. Someone called the attention of Catholic bishop John Martin Henni, who happened to be in Watertown on business, to the unfortunate family, and Bishop Henni came to see the boy for himself. Convinced that this was, indeed, a case for the church, a convocation of Catholic priests was called, of whom Father Minderer of St. Henry's Catholic Church and Father Patrick Pettit of St. Bernard's Catholic Church of Watertown were members, and the catatonic body of Carl Siege was brought to St. Henry's Catholic Church and placed on the altar. The solemn rites of exorcism were begun on a Thursday and didn't end until the following Saturday.

On the first day, four devils were cast out of the unfortunate young man. On Friday, three more were cast out of him, and on Saturday at least one further devil left the body of Carl Siege. The family was so grateful for the help they had been given that they all soon joined the Catholic Church and attended Mass every morning.

Then, about a month after the exorcism, another devil appeared within Carl. It was soon cast out, but not before laughing at the priests and stating that four more devils still resided in the young man. Shortly after this, Carl was committed to the insane department of the Jefferson County Poor House. There he soon began to recover from whatever he may have been suffering from, though it is unknown if he ever fully recovered or, indeed, if he was ever released from the poor house.

The out-of-town newspapers had a field day with this story, and most treated it with a heavy dose of sarcasm. But those who were present at the event knew that this was very real. The Rite of Exorcism is rarely performed by the Catholic Church these days, and it is believed that it may not have been performed in Wisconsin since the Siege case in 1869. Today, the Roman Catholic Church requires doctors to rule out any preexisting medical or psychological conditions before an exorcism is even contemplated.

The Siege case has never been totally forgotten in Watertown, and there is a vague rumor that St. Henry's Catholic Church may be haunted as a result of the event. As local historian and author Kenneth Riedl states in his book, *A Church Built on the Rock: The 150 Year History of St. Henry's Catholic Church*, "Some parishioners say they experience an unexplained chill in the church. Satan doesn't give up easily."

Chapter 9

THE MERRY MINISTERS
OF WATERTOWN

As one reads through this book, it becomes easy to forget that Watertown has a strong religious background, beginning with its earliest settlement. Today, over twenty-five religious denominations are represented in the city. Still, many feel like the man in the 1876 story who was traveling by rail and noticed the skyline of a large city with many church steeples looming in the distance. He called the conductor over and inquired the name of the city. The conductor replied, "Why that's Watertown, our next stop." The man expressed a look of surprise and declared that he couldn't believe it, for he had been made to understand that the only things in Watertown were Germans and breweries.

Most of the early clergymen who served the city were God-fearing men of the cloth. But even the most pious can have feet of clay. With that thought in mind, here are a few stories of Watertown's early clergymen, their foibles and their follies.

Perhaps the most celebrated story of ministerial misconduct concerns Reverend H.B. Heinrichs. He had come to Watertown to serve the congregation of St. Mark's Lutheran Church in 1873. His credentials were somewhat spotty and a little shady, but he had charisma and won over many in the church. But little by little, he began to show odd traits, among them a fondness for strong liquor, and under his leadership certain rules of conduct began to be relaxed. This didn't sit well with the church elders.

They began to investigate his background, and things began to surface that were not to the elders' liking. But there was not enough evidence to have Heinrichs removed from the pulpit. They were looking for something tangible that they could use to have this troublesome pastor removed. Then came the tale of the horse.

There is an apocryphal story about Pastor Heinrichs owning a high-spirited horse that was hard to handle. When the reverend was in his cups, he would let the horse run at will, and people tended to retreat in fear when they saw his buggy coming. One day, so the story goes, Reverend Heinrichs lost control of his horse on Main Street, and the animal charged into the kitchen of Charles Goette's Grocery Store on East Main Street and destroyed a stove. Mr. Goette promptly billed the Board of Elders of St. Mark's for the damage, and the board, in turn, used this as an excuse to terminate Reverend Heinrichs's employment at the church. Sadly, this story cannot be proven, though there was a similar case about this time of the Reverend Dr. Wigginton of Watertown who had a wild horse that ran riot on the city streets. It could be that later historians got the two stories confused, since the records for this time period are missing from the files at St. Mark's. Or was this a convenient coverup for something more sinister? Did Reverend Heinrichs's drinking become a major liability? We may never know for sure.

What is known is that Reverend Heinrichs left town and went down to St. Louis, Missouri, for a time before being called back to Watertown by a number of his followers, former members of St. Mark's. They loved him and wanted him to lead them in the formation of a new church. This church came to be founded in 1875 and is known as Immanuel Lutheran Church.

Sadly, his tenure there was very brief. This was due to his increasing alcoholism. There is a story told of one Sunday when he was conducting a service that his congregation had to sing the same hymn over and over because he had absented himself to indulge in a bit of a morning nip. After a year or so, he realized that he had a problem, so he voluntarily resigned his position at the church he had founded. He left Watertown, and it is believed that he died about 1889.

There are two ministers whose stories bear telling in greater detail. They were both very controversial in their day. One, Christian Sans, has been written of before in various Watertown histories. The other minister though, Karl Wilhelm Ehrenstroem, is a virtual unknown, a mere obscure footnote in the history of the so-called "Old Lutheran" movement in Germany of the 1830s and 1840s. Both men left their mark in the city in one way or another, and both were men of high moral principles and convictions and were

IMMANUEL LUTHERAN CHURCH. This was the church founded by Reverend H. Heinrichs after he was dismissed by St. Mark's Lutheran Church in 1875.

zealous in their desire to spread the Gospel. It is a pity, therefore, that their lives were filled with such turmoil and controversy that it made it impossible for them to have lingered in Watertown for very long.

Christian Sans was from the Westphalia region of Germany, where he received a more liberal education in a German teachers' college. He received no formal theological training except what he studied at the teachers' college, yet his personality was so strong and he exuded such personal magnetism that he was welcomed into many small congregations as a lay minister. He was very highly thought of.

Sans possessed no deep Lutheran beliefs. He was a member of the Franckean Synod, which is today considered part of the Evangelical Lutheran Church of America. This synod was comparatively liberal in its principles. The Franckeans took notice of Sans and decided to send him to

REVEREND CHRISTIAN SANS. One of the most controversial ministers to ever serve a church in Watertown. *Courtesy of St. Mark's Lutheran Church.*

America to minister to their affiliated churches throughout New England. He arrived on American shores in 1839.

He began to serve Lutheran churches in New York State and Pennsylvania. It was while serving in Pennsylvania, in the city of Honesdale, that the first blemish on his character surfaced. While serving there, he was accused of committing the crime of sodomy with several young boys. He strongly declared his innocence, but the public turned against him. No matter how much he tried, he couldn't win them back, so he was forced to leave the area.

He traveled down to New Orleans, Louisiana, where he took charge of a Lutheran church. But a dark cloud seemed to dog his footsteps. The sodomy charge followed him. Worse yet, his church in New Orleans burned down, and he was accused of setting it on fire. Once more, he was compelled to leave his post.

By the early 1850s, he had come to the city of Oshkosh, Wisconsin, where he was lecturing on temperance. In 1853, at the invitation of St. Luke's Lutheran Church, he was called to deliver a test sermon (which was a sort of "audition" for the job) in Watertown. While he was here, he also delivered a

OLD ST. MARK'S CHURCH. Reverend Sans managed to raise the money to have the first brick church in the city erected in 1855. It was demolished in the later 1990s to make way for a new parish hall on this site. *Courtesy of St. Mark's Lutheran Church.*

temperance lecture and made such an impression on the German Lutherans that he was called back in 1854 to help found a brand-new Lutheran church that later became St. Mark's Lutheran Church.

Sans's success as a minister was amazing. He was ahead of his time in many ways. One of his most innovative ideas, for the time, was an English Sunday school, where all ethnic groups could gather to be taught English so that they might assimilate into mainstream culture and also so that English-speaking residents could get to better know their German neighbors.

He cut an imposing figure on the city streets, and he was remembered as having a polite and dignified bearing and long, flowing hair. Sans was, despite his broken English, an eloquent speaker, and he managed to win many friends. Sadly, he also managed to win many enemies, mainly German ones. One unfortunate facet of Sans's personality was his habit of electioneering from the pulpit. He railed against drinking and Sunday picnics in a city where there were five breweries; he tried to influence how his parishioners voted in public elections; and worst of all, he came out in favor of abolition in a heavily Democratic city. Watertown citizens, while not in favor of slavery in principle, were not about to rock the political boat, and

EMIL ROTHE. A newspaper editor and lawyer, he was responsible for stirring up public opinion against Reverend Sans.

most favored the "Little Giant," Stephen A. Douglas, in the coming election over the upstart "Black Republican" Abraham Lincoln. The German leaders of Watertown, headed by newspaper editor Emil Rothe, realized that they had a troublemaker in their midst. Sans, they decided, had to go. But how to do it?

Just then the answer to their problem manifested itself in the person of Reverend Peter Joerris, the minister at St. Luke's Lutheran Church. When Sans first arrived in Watertown, Joerris fell under the charismatic spell of the newcomer and became a willing follower. But something happened to their friendship and they had a falling out. Joerris then began to do some background checking and discovered the ugly stories of sodomy and arson that had been raised against Sans in his previous posts. Joerris turned over his evidence to Rothe, who gleefully printed these charges in the columns of his newspaper, *Der Watertown Weltbuerger*. Over four hundred scandalous articles as well as a slanderous pamphlet were printed by Rothe over a ten-month period, and the citizens of Watertown read them with great interest.

At first, Sans freely admitted to several points, such as his lack of theological training. But he vehemently denied the validity of other points, and finally he was forced to sue Joerris for libel. After two trials, Sans came out victorious, and Joerris was forced to pay all court costs and to apologize publicly.

Unfortunately, by the time of the final ruling, things had gotten very bad for Sans. Criticism of him had reached a fever pitch by the incendiary

COLE'S HALL. Located on the southeast corner of South Second and Main Streets, this is where a mob of anti-Sans people met up with Sans and his supporters and nearly came to blows. *Courtesy of Watertown Historical Society.*

articles in *Der Weltbuerger*, and he had to fear for his life due to his reputation. Mayor C.B. Skinner became Sans's self-appointed protector, and he called a meeting of the anti-Sans faction and read it the riot act. "If shooting some of you is necessary to protect Sans," he told them, "I shall see that it is done!"

Not long after this, some friends of the minister threw him a donation party at John W. Cole's public hall, located on the southeastern corner of South Second and Main Streets. After the festivities were over and as the party was descending the stairs, they were met by an ugly mob of anti-Sans men, who were referred to as "Sons of Belial." Their intent was to throw the minister down the stairs. Mayor Skinner, fighting his way to the front of the crowd, drew his pistol and shouted, "I'll shoot the first man that touches Sans!"

Sans and his supporters made their way out of the hall, and from then on a mayoral-appointed group of vigilantes acted as bodyguards for Sans and his family, following him wherever he went and even taking turns sleeping in his house at night. Officials of the Franckean Synod, which had originally sent Sans to America, stepped in about this time to rule on the matter, and after due deliberation they decided that all of the evidence against Sans, from sodomy to arson, was circumstantial at best and could not be proven. Thus, they exonerated him.

Still, this did not quiet things. There were still disruptive outbreaks regarding the case. Whenever his church congregation got together to discuss the situation, everyone in town would crowd into the church building to listen. These meetings were considered by many to be better entertainment than going to the theatre. These meetings were often disrupted by anti-Sans people, and it got so bad that Carl Schurz, the famed German-American politician (then just starting his career in Watertown), felt compelled to call a meeting of the Germans of Watertown at which he told them to stay out of the business of Sans's church.

Finally, the church board summoned Sans to meet with it to have him publicly answer these charges. Sans refused to do so. The board then had no choice but to dismiss him. He was formally replaced in 1860 by Reverend Johannes Bading, president of the Wisconsin Synod, who quickly wiped away all traces of Christian Sans.

As for the embattled clergyman Sans, he left Watertown and took charge of a large Lutheran congregation in Joliet, Illinois. But misfortune seemed to dog his footsteps, and after serving one church for nearly ten years, he was asked to leave. Undaunted, Sans left, taking with him several families from his former congregation, and founded a new church only a block from his previous one. From time to time he was mentioned in the newspapers here, most notably in the 1870s when, in order to raise money for his Joliet congregation, he was selling photographs of himself! He died in Joliet in 1891. His church in Watertown, St. Mark's Lutheran Church, is today one of the largest Lutheran congregations in the city, and it is thriving.

Finally, we present the strange and sad saga of Pastor Karl Wilhlem Ehrenstroem. His story begins in the former German province of Pomerania, a region in the northeastern part of the former German empire (today considered a part of Poland). At the time he came into prominence, a great religious schism had taken place. Friedrich Wilhelm III, then King of Prussia, had imposed a state-run church upon the people of Pomerania, and this did not sit well with the Lutherans living there. Many Lutheran pastors openly rebelled against the state church, and one of the most opposed to the scheme was Ehrenstroem.

In 1835, he was ordained a Lutheran pastor and served a dozen or so small parishes spread over a wide area. Like others, he suffered much persecution for taking a stand against the state-run church, and he was arrested on eight separate occasions.

Not a great deal is known about Ehrenstroem personally. He was, evidently, much admired by his followers, and they treated him like royalty. When he rode into a town, he often rode in a carriage drawn by six horses, and when he spoke huge crowds flocked to hear him. He was a very charismatic leader, and the many persecutions he suffered gave him an aura of holiness. His preaching, it was claimed, was regarded as if it had come from heaven itself.

By the late 1830s, the Lutherans had had enough of a watered-down religion that was being thrust down their throats. Church leaders began holding meetings to plan for a mass emigration to America, among other places. They wished to go anywhere so that they could worship without government intrusion. Ehrenstroem supported these efforts, and wherever he went he preached emigration.

In 1843, as plans were being finalized for a large immigration to America, Ehrenstroem was once more arrested, this time for libel against the authorities of the government and the leaders of the state-run church. His outspoken ways had done him in. And so, as his followers left on their way to the New World and religious freedom, Ehrenstroem languished, broken-hearted, in a jail cell.

After a year spent in jail and after his wife and others bombarded the Prussian authorities with petitions for his release, Ehrenstroem was freed, and he finally left Prussia. He and his wife arrived in the state of New York, where most of his followers had settled a few months earlier. But misfortune followed him across the sea. Shortly after their arrival, Ehrenstroem's long-suffering wife died. His mind, already affected by his last prison term, became completely unhinged, and it was said that he tried, in vain, to resurrect his wife from the dead. When that proved fruitless, he took her body with him to upstate New York, where he had been called to serve a church, and had her buried beneath a chicken coop.

Ehrenstroem was clearly delusional by this time, and at a mass meeting of his flock he proclaimed that he could and would do miracles among them. He promised that under his teaching they, too, would be able to perform miracles. The younger members of his congregation were mesmerized and followed him blindly, while the older members just shook their heads in disbelief.

Ehrenstroem then instituted a rigid program of prayer exercises that included, among other things, the forced shouting of prayers. These sessions dragged on for such interminable lengths of time that many of his followers often fell into a trancelike state and some even had seizures or fits. These fits, Ehrenstroem declared, were the signs of a true believer. He also imposed twenty-four-hour fasts for his minions and their livestock.

Things got progressively worse. Ehrenstroem, clearly deranged and suffering from a messiah complex, now felt it was time to perform a miracle. There was a blind man known to many in the town where Ehrenstroem had his church. He and his followers selected him for their miracle. Through the power of prayer, they would restore his sight. But after a lengthy session of intense prayer, ardent exhortation and stern commands, the man remained blind.

Many of his followers now began to lose their trust in him and left him. Those who remained were now subjected to even harsher (and stranger) rules. Ehrenstroem rejected the German Bible and the teachings of Martin Luther, and he ordered his followers to learn Greek so that they could read the Bible as it was originally written. He demanded that his followers gather up all their German books of religious instruction, including their Bibles, and he had a public book burning. Ehrenstroem even demanded that his male followers should allow their hair and beards to grow long, like the disciples of Christ did. He, himself, wore as his vestments a flowing robe and, incongruously, Wellington boots.

Church officials back in upstate New York had their fill of this oddball, and they excommunicated Ehrenstroem and suspended him from the ministry for teaching false doctrine. But this did not stop him. Determined to go where he and his followers could worship as they pleased, he gathered what remained of his flock, and they set out for Wisconsin. On their way they ran into another obstacle: Lake Michigan. Undeterred, Ehrenstroem raised his hands like Moses and attempted to part the waters so that he and his flock could pass through undisturbed. Needless to say, the effort didn't succeed.

Ehrenstroem and his followers arrived in Milwaukee, and he sent out parties to search the area for likely spots to set up a new communal community. His scouts reported back that they had found a congenial spot in Watertown. They arrived in the city in September 1845. They had managed to obtain, sight unseen, a half-finished frame building owned by local druggist Dr. Edward Johnson. This building was located on the site of what is today the Town and Country Bank, on the north side of West Main next to the Rock River. But when Ehrenstroem and his hairy, wild-eyed followers arrived and Dr. Johnson got a good look at them, he got a bit spooked and refused to let them have the property.

After much running around, the little group finally managed to rent a building from John W. Cole, a pioneer businessman. This building was little more than a stable, and while they could sleep inside it, they had to set up a stove outside the place in order to do their cooking and baking. While in the city, they actively continued searching for a more suitable place to set up their new community. They found it in the vicinity of nearby Lebanon to the north of Watertown.

There they managed to buy roughly eighty acres of land on which they lived as a communal society. They built a large house for themselves consisting of one large room where they all lived together. The Ehrenstroem party at this time consisted of three married couples and their children, three unmarried men and three unmarried women. Ehrenstroem acted as the head of the family.

The group continued its study of Greek, and the men grew their hair and beards even longer. Ehrenstroem, just as crazy here as he was back east, promised his followers that they could go out among the wild animals that abounded in the countryside as naked as Adam and Eve and the people would be unharmed. It is unknown if this attempt at nudism ever took place, but it would have certainly raised more than a few eyebrows of the staid Germans and God-fearing Yankees who lived in the area.

All seemed to be going well for the little community. And then disaster struck. Just after Ehrenstroem and his followers had improved their land and put in a crop, it was discovered that they had settled on the wrong property! A surveyor came out from Milwaukee to check the property lines, and it was discovered that the Ehrenstroem property was actually about a mile south of where they had settled. So they were obliged to start all over again.

Interestingly enough, the land that the Ehrenstroem party had originally settled on was purchased by one of his followers, "Squire" Charles Beckmann. He was a bit of an eccentric character and known for his little quirks. For example, he always walked wherever he went and carried a cane in his right hand and an umbrella under his arm. He smoked a long-stemmed pipe, the bowl of which was always held in his left hand. Beckmann was highly esteemed by those who knew him, and he served a number of public offices, including a term as mayor of Watertown in 1868. He died in Watertown in 1892.

With the prospect of having to start all over from scratch, the Ehrenstroem communal living community broke up. His followers left him, many founding the Lebanon Baptist Church. Others returned to the state of New York. As for their leader, he was now a broken man. Ehrenstroem left Watertown and

SQUIRE CHARLES BECKMANN. A one-time follower of Reverend Ehrenstroem, Beckmann ultimately bought the property that housed the failed communal living experiment. He later served a term as mayor of Watertown. *Courtesy of* Watertown Daily Times.

returned to New York himself and worked for a time as a language teacher. He later tried to gather a group to travel to the gold fields in California in hopes of funding a new church. Sadly, his luck was no better there, and he died in abject poverty in California about 1852. Ehrenstroem was quickly forgotten by his followers and by the religious order he had worked so feverishly to sustain. A sad end to a man whose life held so much promise.

SELECT BIBLIOGRAPHY

Butterfield, C.W. *The History of Jefferson County, Wisconsin.* Chicago: Western Publishing Co., 1879.

Camann, Eugene W. *Uprooted From Prussia—Transplanted in America.* Buffalo, NY: Gilcraft Printing Co., 1991.

Colonius, H.C. "Geschichte von Watertown, nach mundlichen Uberliefungen." Serially in *Der Watertown Weltbuerger*, beginning September 26, 1868. Reprinted in the same newspaper beginning April 15, 1905.

Democratic State Register. March 12, 1850–November 4, 1854.

Harger's Times. January 5, 1878–September 7, 1878.

Jacobi, C. Hugo. "Reminiscences of Early Days in Watertown." Serially in the *Watertown Daily Times*, beginning February 1, 1924. Original articles in German in *Der Watertown Weltbuerger*, serially beginning May 5, 1923.

Jannke, William F., III. *150 Years Living the Word: A History of St. Mark's Evangelical Lutheran Church, Watertown, Wisconsin 1854–2004.* Watertown, WI: Bethesda Print Shop, 2006.

————. *Robbers, Rascals & Ruffians: A Bus Tour of Watertown's Dark Side.* Watertown, WI: privately printed, 1997.

————. *Watertown, A History.* Charleston, SC: Arcadia Publishing, 2002.

Jefferson County Clerk of Court Records. 1839–1936. Currently held by the Dodge-Jefferson Genealogical Society.

Moen, Bill, and Doug Davis. *Badger Bars and Tavern Tales: An Illustrated History of Wisconsin Saloons.* Woodruff, WI: Guest Cottage, 2003.

Mueller, Mary (Beggan). *The Beggans of Watertown: Some Stuff You Never Knew.* Watertown, WI: privately printed, 1995.

Riedl, Kenneth M. *A Church Built on the Rock: The 150-Year History of St. Henry's Catholic Church, Watertown, Wisconsin 1853–2003.* Madison, WI: Omnipress Printing Co., 2003.

————. *Watertown Fire Department 1857–2007.* Watertown, WI: Hometown Series of Publications, 2007.

Watertown Chronicle. June 30, 1847–October 9, 1856.

Watertown Daily Times. November 23, 1895–present.

Watertown Democrat. October 26, 1854–February 22, 1883.

Watertown Gazette. July 22, 1879–March 18, 1937.

Watertown Republican. April 24, 1867–April 6, 1906.

Whyte, Dr. William F. "Chronicles of Early Watertown." *Wisconsin Magazine of History*, March 1921.